How To Get Your Motorcycle Up & Running

The
Shop Manual
For All
Years Makes and Models

By Leigh & Randy Ellis

TX 6 - 604 - 184 Dated 7/10/07

ISBN # 0 - 97 - 5877 - 2 - 24

Layout & Design by Studio 5   www.studio5design.net

L & R Publishing
P.O. Box 3081
Everett, WA 98203
www.getitrunning.com

Table of Contents

Preface

Section I.

Table of Contents (cont.)

Section II.

Table of Contents (cont.)

Table of Contents (cont.)

How To Get Your Motorcycle Up & Running

The
Shop Manual
For All
Years Makes and Models

By Leigh & Randy Ellis

Preface

So, you have a motorcycle that's been sitting in your garage for years ….or, you've been given a motorcycle by a friend or relative and "it just needs a little TLC to run again"….or, you found a motorcycle at a garage sale that you picked up for a song. But it doesn't run. And the local motorcycle dealership won't work on it because "it's too old" and the shops that WILL work on it want a small fortune to make it run. So, what do you do?

Well, you have three options. You can pay the shop that WILL work on it, and spend hundreds, or thousands of dollars getting it running and putting it in reliable working order. Or, you can say "To hell with that! I'll just junk it!" Or, you can buy this book and learn how to make your motorcycle run yourself. Yes, you can! With this how to manual, along with the service manual for your particular, year, make and model of bike, you can make your motorcycle run!

We explain how to make your motorcycle run in easy to understand non-technical language, and we even explain how to get a service manual to use for free. With service manuals costing in the neighborhood of $20.00 to $50.00, that's a valuable piece of information we pass along to you.

Now the reason we've written this book, is because over the past twenty years of owning our own repair shop, we've answered literally thousands of questions from people just like yourself explaining "how to" procedures. A lot of times we've given customers enough information over the telephone so they could get their bikes running well enough to drive into our shop for further work.

The reason most motorcycles have to have a "make-run" procedure done, is because they've just been setting too long without being run. Hey, if you don't use it, you lose it!

Section I. of this manual will take you step by step through the three secrets of getting your motorcycle up and running. Section II. will cover all of the other problems motorcycles have that are caused by prolonged setting. Remember – use it or lose it! Section III. will teach you how to keep your motorcycle running so it will always start. We will also explain the winterizing steps you need to follow so your bike will start and run in the spring.

Now, let's get down to business. Let's get that bike of yours up and running, and we'll see you on the open road!

Leigh

Leigh Ellis

Chapter 1

Introduction

Overview of This Book

Okay, you've spent your money on this book – now here is how to get the most out of it and make it work for you. This book is designed to <u>help you get your motorcycle up and running</u> and keep it running.

At first glance, a motorcycle looks complicated but it's not, at least not as far as a make-run procedure goes. The make-run procedure is a three-step process of how to get your motorcycle running. You <u>don't</u> need hundreds of dollars worth of tools, and you <u>don't need</u> an engineering degree to get your motorcycle up and running. All you need is a few hand tools, this book and the service manual for your particular bike.

1. **Read the introduction and all the overviews first.**
2. Familiarize yourself with this book and your service manual, so you will know where to go when you need information specific to your particular bike.
3. Make sure you read and understand all the safety instructions in the service manual for your particular motorcycle.
4. If you don't have a service manual, read "Your Service Manual" in this book on how to get a service manual to use for free.

Our attitude is <u>YOU CAN</u> get your motorcycle up and running with the help of this book. If your attitude is the same, then your success is a given!

Please , Just Tell Me What To Do !

Confused ? Don't Worry !
We Will Take You Step By Step Through The
Make-Run Process !

Your Service Manual

Because of the differences between years, makes and models, along with this book, you will also need a service manual for your particular motorcycle. This book and your service manual will work together as a team to help you get your motorcycle running.

If, for some reason, you don't know what year, make and model of bike you have, you can find this out by writing down the frame number. This is the motorcycle identification number, and you should be able to find it on a plate welded onto the frame, either on the neck of the bike or on the side. Call the dealership that sells your brand of bike. Ask to speak to someone in the parts department; give them the frame number and ask them to look up the year and model. Once you have the year, make and model, purchase a service manual for your bike from your dealer.

If you don't want to buy one, you can go to your local library. Tell the librarian what service manual you want. Eighty percent of the time your library won't have your service manual but that isn't a problem because there is such a thing as the Inter-Library Loan system.

You have a better than eighty percent chance that your service manual is out there in some other library – and you can get it on loan by just asking for it at your library. If your service manual is in any library in the U.S., Canada, Europe or Asia, you can get it through the inter-library loan system. Usually there is no charge; you can keep it for two weeks, and you can get an extension for another two weeks.

Once you get your service manual, study it and start thinking of your motorcycle as a two-wheeled training aid. Whatever you learn about your motorcycle will translate to all other motorcycles. Read and understand all the safety tips in your service manual. The service manual for your motorcycle has priority over this book when it comes to safety concerns.

Don't be intimidated by everything that is in the service manual because most of what's in your service manual doesn't have a thing to do with getting your motorcycle running. You do <u>not need</u> to know all the engineering details about how your bike works in order to get it running.

Your advantage is that you only have one motorcycle to learn about. With this book, and less than ten percent of what's in your service manual, you can get your motorcycle running, and we will send you to your service manual when you need to get some specific information about your bike.

Rule of Thumb

Never take your motorcycle into a shop for repairs just before you plan to sell it. You will never get back the money that you spent. You are better off fixing it yourself, or giving the buyer a break on the price and letting them fix it.

How a Motorcycle's Engine Works

For details of how your particular engine works, see your service manual.

What a motorcycle's engine does is the same for all bikes. How it does it, is different depending on the year, make and model. A motorcycles engine needs just three things to start and run.

The first thing it needs is compression. If you don't have enough compression, the fuel/air mixture will not explode with enough energy to start and run the bike. If you take a little gasoline and pour it on the ground and light it, you don't get an explosion - you get a fire. Why? Because it was not compressed with air; this is what happens inside a motorcycle engine that does not have enough compression to run; the gas just burns and does not explode.

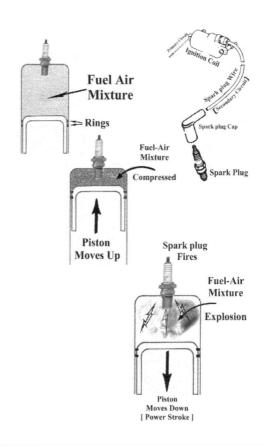

The second thing your bike needs is a timed hot spark. The spark ignites the fuel/air mixture that the piston has compressed. This causes an explosion that pushes the piston back through the cylinder. If you have a hot timed spark and compression, the fuel will explode.

The third thing you need is the right mixture of fuel and air. The fuel (gas) and the air need to be mixed in the right ratio so the fuel will explode. This is the job of the carburetor. If there is too little gas to air, your motor will run "hot" (lean) and may do damage to the motor. If there is too much gas to air, your bike will run "rich", fouling your spark plugs.

In a Nut-Shell

When you have compression, a timed hot spark, and the right fuel/air mixture all at the same time, you will get an explosion that will start and run the motorcycle.

A motorcycle's engine is designed to make these controlled fuel/air explosions. It then uses these explosions to drive the motorcycle forward and to run all the power systems on the bike.

Did You Know That?

A motorcycle's engine is only about 20% efficient. This means that only 20% of the energy made by the exploding fuel/air mixture is used to push the motorcycle forward. The other 80% is wasted as heat and friction.

Chapter 2

Compression

Overview on Compression

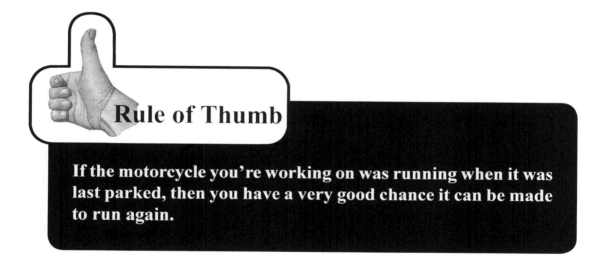

Rule of Thumb

If the motorcycle you're working on was running when it was last parked, then you have a very good chance it can be made to run again.

A motorcycle engine needs explosions to get it running and keep it running. You get these explosions when the motor compresses the fuel/air mixture and ignites it repeatedly.

Compression brings the oxygen in the air and the fuel together in a confined space under pressure. The more pressure, fuel, and air, the more powerful the explosion.

Your motor has to have enough compression to explode the fuel/air mixture. The magic number is 100 psi (pounds per square inch); without this magic 100 psi minimum of compression, your motor will not start and run. Compression is usually, "Do me first."

The only way to know that you have at least 100 psi is to do a compression test. The compression test will tell you exactly how much compression each cylinder has. As a rule of thumb, a motor needs 125 to 150 psi to run right but you don't need to worry about that now. You just want to know if you have the minimum of 100 psi that it takes to get your motorcycle up and running.

Did You Know That?

If you put your thumb over the spark plug hole and crank over the bike, your thumb can only hold 30 to 50 pounds of pressure.

The Compression Test

The first thing to do in testing for compression is to check the oil level. If the oil level is low, fill it with the right amount of oil. See your service manual for how to check your oil and at what level it should be.

If there is too much oil in the motorcycle, drain out the excess and make sure there is no gas mixed with the oil. This can happen if the gas is left on and the carburetor overflows letting fuel into the combustion chamber. This fuel then drains past the rings into the crankcase mixing with the oil. If your oil looks thin and runny, it probably has gas mixed in with it.

If the oil looks white and milky, its probably got water mixed in with it. So when in doubt – throw it out! Drain all your oil out of the crankcase and/or transmission. Check the "how to change your oil" in your motorcycle service manual and change the oil and filter. If you have gas or water mixed with your oil, then you will also have gas or water in the oil filter and possibly in the air filter as well.

Next, remove all the spark plugs. Take your time and get them out without breaking them off. This could be a real bear of a job, so be careful.

The reason it could be difficult to remove the spark plugs is because of a term called electrolysis. No, we don't mean removing excess body hair. In this case, we're referring to a chemical reaction. This is one of those technical terms we don't want to use a lot of but we have to here.

Electrolysis is just a fancy way of saying "Hey guys! You've left us (the spark plugs) in here too damned long!" They're attempting to weld themselves in place.

Once you have the spark plugs out, install a compression gauge into the spark plug hole. There are two kinds of compression gauges available, both are shown here. One is a screw in type and one is a press in type.

Safety Tip

Get the spark plug wires out of your way, so you won't get an electric spark-shark attack. If you don't do this first, you may be shocked with 20,000 to 60,000 volts – not a good thing!

Also, think what will happen if there is gas in the combustion chamber and you turn the engine over and the gas comes out under pressure and hits the spark plug wire just as it is sparking. Yes, a flame-thrower in your face you have made! Don't let this happen, even if you have to disable the motorcycle from sparking. This can be done by disconnecting the wire(s) that go to the coil.

If you have an electric starter, make sure that your battery is in good shape and fully charged.

Note: If the bike only has an electric starter, and the bike doesn't crank over, go to the Chapter 9 on Electric Starter Systems; also see your service manual for details on your particular starter system layout.

When it is safe, open the throttle wide and crank the engine over until you get at least 100 psi. Your motorcycle will run with 100 psi, it will run well with 125 psi, and it will run great with 150 to 180 psi. But for now, you just need 100 psi to get it started.

Look at the compression gauge and see what reading you're getting. If it's at least 100 psi or better, great! Now repeat this process for each cylinder you have. If you have 100 psi or better on all your cylinders, you're finished with the compression test and you need to move on to Chapter 3 on Spark.

If you do not have at least 100 psi on all cylinders, go to Troubleshooting Compression.

Troubleshooting Compression

If your motorcycle engine doesn't have at least 100 psi on all cylinders, then there is something wrong and it will need to be taken care of before going any further. Without at least 100 psi, a motorcycle will not start and run right.

The basic rule of thumb is, if your motorcycle was running before it was left setting, you should be able to make it run again. If the engine turns over, but the compression reading is less than 100 psi in one or more cylinders, your motor has a problem. Check your service manual to see if you have a two or a four stroke motor.

Two Stroke Motors

If you have a two stroke motor, and you have low compression, you either have a hole in the piston (if your compression reading is less than 10 psi) or the rings are stuck or worn out. Hopefully, they're just stuck from setting.

Oil Test

Add a tablespoon of motor oil in through the spark plug hole and re-do the compression test. If the compression goes up above 100 psi of the cylinder that has low compression and stays up, then you have loosened up the rings and they should stay sealed. If so, move on to Chapter 3 on Spark.

If the compression goes up above 100 and then drops below 100 psi, then the rings have not sealed and may need replacing. But before you replace the rings by rebuilding the top end, try using a product called "Power Tune Engine Cleaner" (a trade secret). You can find it at any Mercury Marine dealership. Shoot it down the spark plug hole and then crank the motor over. It also helps to leave the engine cleaner in the motor overnight. If the compression comes up, and stays up on all cylinders using the engine cleaner, then move on to Chapter 3 on Spark.

If you get the compression up over 80 but not up to 100 psi, then do a oil /gas start technique. (See this chapter). If you have a multiple cylinder bike that has at least one cylinder that is over 100 psi you can try a hot/cold start technique. (See this chapter).

Four Stroke Motors

Read about two stroke motors first.

Four stroke motors have rings like two strokes, plus intake and exhaust valves. On four strokes you will have to determine if it is rings or valves that is causing the lack of compression.

Oil Test

Take a tablespoon of motor oil and pour it into the spark plug hole. Repeat the compression test this way for each cylinder that has less than 100 psi.

When you re-do the compression test with oil in the combustion chamber, one of three things is going to happen on four stroke bikes.

1. The oil will temporarily seal the rings and loosen them up so they will stay sealed even after the oil has been worked out. The compression will go up and

stay up over the magic 100 psi. This should be true for all the cylinders. If so, you're finished with the compression trouble shooting. Go to Chapter 3 on Spark.

2. The compression will go up over 100 psi, and then drop below 100 psi when the oil is worked out, leaving you under the minimum 100 psi compression you need. This means that the rings are worn out or hopefully, just stuck from setting too long. Try using the "Power Tune Engine Cleaner" in a can described in two strokes above.

If, after using "Power Tune Engine Cleaner", if the compression reading is at least 100 psi. for all cylinders, then go on to Chapter 3 on Spark.

If the "Power Tune Engine Cleaner" does not get the compression up to 100 psi, there are just two things left to try before you consider rebuilding your engine. You can do an oil/gas start test (see this chapter). If you have a multiple cylinder motor with at least one cylinder over 100 psi, you can start it on just one cylinder and let the heat get the other rings to re-seal. (See hot/cold starting in this chapter).

3. If the compression stays the same and doesn't go up at all, then you have one of two possible problems. Your valves may be burned or out of adjustment on the tight side, or you may have a hole in your piston.

Valve Adjustment on Four Strokes That Have Low Compression on the Oil Test

If the compression does not go up when the rings are sealed with oil, then it is most likely that your valves are causing the low compression reading.

Look in your service manual and find out how to check your valve clearance. First, do a valve clearance test to determine if your valves are too tight. This is done with a feeler gauge. If valves are too tight, they will let the fuel/air mixture out of the combustion chamber past the intake or exhaust valves. This causes low compression.

If your valves are out of adjustment on the tight side, you will need to adjust them. How to do a valve adjustment is different for most years, makes and models of motorcycles. Some motorcycle valves are mechanically adjusted, using a feeler gauge and some hand tools. Some are adjustable, using small disks called shims and shim replacement tools. Some are not adjustable at all – they're hydraulic.

The first thing you need to determine is if your motorcycle has adjustable valves. (Check your service manual). If they are adjustable, check to see which kind they are; adjustable mechanically, or shim type.

Once you know which type of valves you have, you will need to get a feeler gauge and the tools you will need to adjust the valves. See your service manual for the details. You can get these tools through the dealership that sells your model of motorcycle. If you have shim type valves, you can also trade your old shims in for new shims of the right thickness. Expect a charge per shim exchanged.

If you find that your valves are too tight, adjust them and re-check the compression. Did you get the magic 100 psi?. If not, you will need to rebuild the top end of your motorcycle because the valves are burnt or damaged. If the compression comes up over 100 psi on all cylinders after the valve adjustment, then you're done with compression troubleshooting. Move on to Chapter 3 – Spark.

Oil/Gas Start Technique

We invented this technique along with the "hot and cold starting technique", so that you could give a motorcycle a last ditch effort to start and run.

You can try the oil/gas start technique, if you have at least 100 psi with oil, but then it drops below 100 psi once the oil has worked out of the cylinder. You will have already determined that the low compression is due to sticking rings and not valves, (see oil test above); if this is the case, you can try this technique. You also need to have your spark and fuel systems working right before trying this. See Chapter 3 on Spark and Chapter 6 on Fuel Systems.

The oil/gas start technique allows you to try to start the bike even though it may not have 100 psi without oil. In order to do this technique, you add a tablespoon of oil through the spark plug hole to get the compression up over 100 psi by temporarily sealing the rings. Then you add half a teaspoon of gas on top of the oil so you don't need to choke the bike. Do this for each cylinder. Next, put in a <u>new spark plug</u>.

If you have a bike with a kick lever, you will need to push the bike to get the pistons moving fast enough to build up compression. The best way to do this is to run it downhill with a friend or two pushing.

Put the bike in second or third gear and get it going and then let the clutch out. The motor will turn over and the compression will go up over 100 psi. The engine will start and this will make heat that should help in re-seating the rings.

When the bike starts, try to keep it running to build up the heat. The longer it runs, the more likely it will be that the rings will re-seat. Repeat this technique as many times as necessary. Keep doing this as long as you see progress. If you have a bike with an electric starter, you can do this technique by cranking the bike over instead of pushing it.

Safety Tip

Do not pull the bike behind a vehicle. It can kill you!

Hot/Cold Starting Technique

If you have a multiple cylinder motor that has at least one cylinder with 100 psi of compression without adding oil down the cylinder, you can do what we call <u>a hot/cold starting technique</u>. You can give a motorcycle a very good chance of running again with this technique, provided that you know that the compression is low due to rings not seating properly.

Before you do this technique, you need to have a hot spark that is timed right and the fuel system needs to be in good shape. (See Chapter 3 on Spark and Chapter 6 on Fuel Systems.)

The goal is to get the motor running on just one or more cylinders that have at least 100 psi. As the heat from the first cylinder moves through the engine, it should get the other cylinder rings to re-seat. As each cylinder gets to 100 psi, add a new spark plug so it can start running and make even more heat. Keep this up until all the cylinders are up to 100 psi or better and they are all running.

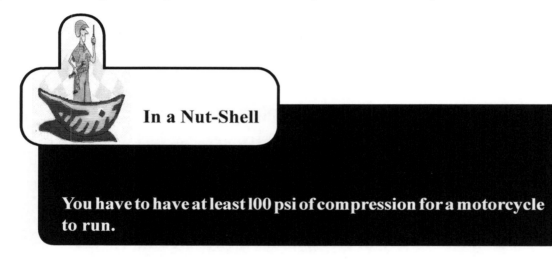

In a Nut-Shell

You have to have at least 100 psi of compression for a motorcycle to run.

Chapter 3

Spark

Overview on Spark

The second step to getting your motorcycle up and running is determining if your motor has "spark". What is spark? Spark is a high voltage current jumping an air gap at the tip of the spark plug.

This man-made lightening strike is used to ignite the fuel/air mixture that has been compressed to at least 100 psi. When this happens, the fuel/air mixture explodes, causing a high pressure that pushes the piston back through the cylinder changing the chemical energy of the fuel into mechanical energy that is used to drive the motorcycle forward.

The spark has to be properly timed to the movement of the piston and the speed of the engine. This is because the fuel/air explosion expands at the same speed all the time, no matter how fast the motor is going.

In order for the fuel/air mixture explosion to keep up with the increasing engine speed, the fuel/air mixture needs to be ignited sooner. When the engine slows down, the spark timing needs to be slowed down (retarded) to correspond to a slower running engine. Motorcycle spark timing is controlled by it's ignition system.

Rule of Thumb

If the motor turns over but doesn't start, then you have a 99% chance it's the compression, spark, or the fuel system that is the problem.

If you don't have spark, you will have to learn how to troubleshoot your particular spark ignition system. You won't have to learn all there is to know about all the different spark ignition systems there are on all the different motorcycles out there – just the one that you have on your bike. Your advantage is that you can learn just the one ignition system on the bike you're working on.

Now, there are two types of ignition systems used in motorcycles: a battery-fired ignition system and a magneto-fired system. Most street bikes use a battery-fired system and most dirt bikes use a magneto-fired system. Look in your service manual to determine if your motorcycle is battery-fired or magneto-fired.

A battery-fired ignition system uses a battery for the current source to fire the spark. It does this by using either a set of points or an electronic ignition system, depending on the year, make and model of motorcycle. Most street bike models manufactured after 1980 are electronic ignition, TPI (transistorized pointless ignition) systems, or CDI (capacitor discharge ignition) systems.

A magneto-fired ignition system uses a magneto for the current source to fire the spark. The magneto-fired system is used mainly on dirt bikes, duel sports, and all terrain vehicles. The magneto-fired ignition system is used in combination with either points or a CDI (capacitor discharge ignition) system, depending again on the year, make and model of motorcycle.

In a Nut-Shell

You have to have a hot timed spark to explode the compressed air/gas mixture.

How To Do a Spark Test

The spark test is as simple as A.B.C.

A. Do you have spark?
B. Is the spark strong enough to fire the compressed fuel/air mixture?
C. Is the spark properly timed and advancing?

Let's find out

1. Remove the spark plugs from the motor.

2. Put the spark jump test tool (that you have made – see Chapter 12 on Tools) into the spark plug cap.

3. Ground the spark jump test tool by connecting the clamp to a good ground, ie., the side of the engine.

4. Crank the bike over, as if you are trying to start it.

5. You should see a spark jump from the center of the test tool to the outer ring.

6. As the bike cranks, the spark should repeat in a consistent manner.

7. If you have spark jumping from the center of the test tool to the outer ring, then you know that you have spark. You also know that the spark is strong enough to fire the compressed fuel/air mixture.

8. Repeat this test for every cylinder.

9. If you have a repetitive spark that jumped the test tool, then go to your service manual and find the chapter on spark timing and make sure that your timing is correct. If not, adjust your timing as your service manual indicates. Some electronic ignition bikes do not have an adjustable spark timing or advance, but are pre-set at the factory and can't be changed, but check it anyway. The timing advance can be different for different years, makes and models.

10. Once you have spark, and the spark timing and the advance are working properly, you are finished with spark. Now, go on to Chapter 6 on Fuel.

If you still have no spark, then remove the spark plug caps, and replace them with new ones. Most unscrew, but some need to be cut off. If you cut, make sure that you leave enough spark plug lead to reach the tops of the spark plugs.

After you replace the spark plug caps, re-do the spark test. If you have spark now, then go to Chapter 6 on Fuel. If you still don't have spark, then go to the Overview of Ignition Systems, (see below), and then on to Troubleshooting Ignition Systems.

Overview on Ignition Systems

Before you start troubleshooting your ignition system, you need to study and understand the ignition system in your service manual. You do NOT need to be an expert on every ignition system there is, but you do need to be an expert on YOUR ignition system – and on troubleshooting your ignition system. It's a lot easier to figure out what's wrong when you know how your ignition system is supposed to work.

Take your time, and study your service manual and this manual until you understand what to do. This manual will help you get a good handle on your ignition system, but your service manual should give you more details on troubleshooting your individual system.

If you need to do a resistance check, then check the specifications in your service manual for your particular bike.

The tools you will need to troubleshoot your ignition system are readily available, and you don't need all the tools on the planet. If you don't have all the tools you need, then buy just the tools you need to get the job done.

You're trading time; your time for the money – the money you would have spent at a repair shop. So buy good tools because they're cheap in the long run. Now it's time to find out how your ignition system works.

Go to your service manual and read the chapter on your ignition system, both how it works and how to troubleshoot it. Then come back here and find your system. With the knowledge from your service manual and this book, you will be able to troubleshoot your ignition system.

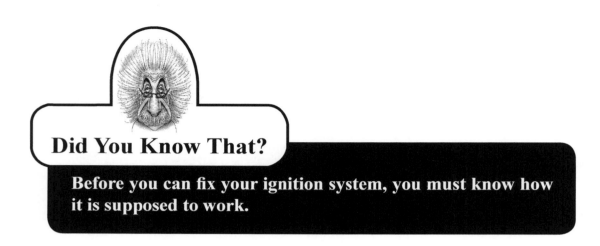

Did You Know That?

Before you can fix your ignition system, you must know how it is supposed to work.

Troubleshooting Electrical Wiring and Components

Your colour code and wiring schematics are in your service manual along with all your electrical component tests. Also, read the 80/20 rule of electrical tests.

If you have a good battery great; if not replace it before doing the electrical tests. Our attitude when it comes to wiring and electrical component troubleshooting, is for you to learn all there is to know about your particular motorcycle's wiring system before you start to fix it.

You have just one wiring system, and on motorcycles it's usually on the outside of the frame where you can get to it. Don't cut into the wiring harness, unless it is absolutely necessary. It's better to go around the problem, than to start cutting away at the harness.

If you blow fuses, then you have a short or an overload on your system.

If some component doesn't work, then it is either out of the circuit, (not getting positive and/or negative), or it is bad. Go to your service manual and read the chapter on your ignition system, both how it works and how to trouble shoot it. Then come back here and find your system.

If some component stays on all the time, then it's control switch is bad, or there is a wire touching ground after the component that is completing the circuit to ground.

That is all that can be wrong with a wiring and component system. Take your time and learn how your system works.

If you don't have a basic understanding of electricity and electrical wiring and components, get the book, "There Are No Electrons". This is a great beginners introduction to how electricity works.

Use Only The Best Electrical Terminal Connectors. Yes, They Cost More But They Keep Working When The Cheaper Ones Quit

You Can Get Them As Individuals or in Kits at The Dealership That Sells Your Make of Bike

The 80/20 Rule

When doing electrical tests, you need to understand that there is an 80/20 rule to testing motorcycle electrical components.

This 80/20 rule says that if you have an electrical problem and you test an electrical component and it tests "good", the odds are that you have an 80% chance that it is indeed "good". But you also have a 20% chance that it's "bad"!

You can also invert this rule to say if testing an electrical component and it tests "bad", then you have an 80% chance that it is "bad", but you also have a 20% chance that it is "good".

How do you know for sure? There is only one way, and that is to replace the suspected bad component with a known good one. What is a "known good electrical component"? A brand-new, out of the box, electrical component is considered to be a "good" component. But (just to confuse you further) sometimes it's not.

A real known good electrical component is a component that does what it is supposed to do! When it is in use. And it keeps doing what it's supposed to do over a period of time.

A known good electrical component can be a component off of a motorcycle just like yours that works on the bike you're taking it off of and it works on your bike too.

Another way to test your suspected "bad" component, is to place it on a motorcycle just like yours and see if it does what it's supposed to do on this other bike over a period of time.

As you can see, my point is, that replacement is the only true test of a suspected bad electrical component. By replacing it with a known "good" component, you can then know for sure if the component you suspect is truly at fault.

In a Nut-Shell

An electrical component can test "good", and be "bad". It can test "bad" and be "good". The only way to know for sure, is to replace the component with a known "good" one.

The Rotating Magnet Coil

Before we get into magnetos and signal generators, you need to understand rotating magnets and what happens when a rotating magnet goes past a coil of wire.

When a rotating magnet passes close to a coil of wire (as seen above), an electrical current is made in the coil of wire. This electrical current then moves through the wire to a location where it is used. The faster the magnet moves past the coil, the stronger will be the electrical pulse.

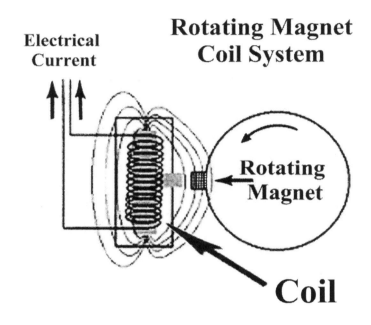

Rotating Magnet Coil System

Electrical Current

Rotating Magnet

Coil

In a magneto fired ignition system, the magnet and the coil are designed to make enough current to fire an ignition coil. A smaller current is needed when the current is used as a signal generator for timing an electronic ignition system.

This same system is used to make current in a charging system, to recharge a battery, or in a non-battery lighting system to power the lights.

It does not matter how big or small the rotating magnets and coil are; they all work the same way. Their job is to produce a pulse of electric current that is used by the system that they're part of.

Another way to think about a rotating magnet/coil system, is that the magnet and coil work together as a pump. This pump then changes the mechanical energy of the turning magnet into electrical current that is pumped through the wires to a location where this current is used.

The current that comes from a coil magnet system is always A.C. (alternating current). If your bike needs D.C (direct current), then your bike will have a diode system called a rectifier that will change the A.C. to D.C.

Did You Know That?

The rotating magnet coil is used on motorcycles for charging batteries, running lighting, and powering and tripping electronic ignition systems.

Chapter 4

Points Ignition Systems

Overview of Battery-Fired Ignition Systems With Points

This system has a battery as a power source and a set of cam driven points that work as a switch to control when the spark fires.

Battery fired ignition systems with points also have a condenser to reduce sparking at the points and a coil (transformer) to convert the battery's voltage to higher voltage that is capable of jumping the air gap at the spark plug.

This system also has an ignition switch that turns the electrical power on and off.

Rule of Thumb

When in doubt, throw them out – spark plugs, spark plug caps, old gas, old oil, and old points and condensers. It's better to throw them out, than waste your time trying to get them to work.

How the Battery Fired Ignition System With Points Works

The ignition switch is turned on. The current goes to the ground of the motorcycle through the negative ground wire. Most motorcycles have a negative ground; if yours has a positive ground, then the current travels in the opposite direction, but it is tested the same way as shown here.

The current travels through the negative grounded frame and then through the motor to the fixed points and to the condenser.

The current travels through the fixed breaker point to the movable breaker point (if they are closed), to the ignition coil, then through the ignition coil and the ignition switch and fuse to the positive side of the battery.

When the current goes through the ignition coil, it activates the primary circuit in the coil and energizes the secondary circuit; at this time the coil is ready to fire.

As the breaker cam (the cam can be located on the end of the valve cam or on the end of the crankshaft) turns, it opens the points.

When the points open, it opens (breaks) the circuit from ground to the coil.

Breaking the coil circuit causes the coils energy to collapse. This collapsing of the coil energy sends a high voltage surge through the secondary circuit to the spark plugs.

When this high voltage current gets to the spark plug, the current wants to complete its circuit to ground and back to the battery. It will do this if the current is powerful enough to jump the air gap at the spark plug, making a spark in the process. This spark fires the fuel/air mixture that has been compressed to at least 100 psi. By repeating this process, the motorcycle starts and continues to run.

Variations on the Battery Fired Ignition Circuit With Points

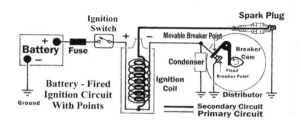

The above diagram is for a single cylinder motorcycle. The battery fired ignition circuit with points has been set up on singles, twins, triples, and four cylinder motorcycles; mostly on street and on/off road bikes before 1980.

There are differences between years, makes and models. See your motorcycle service manual for the details. For instance, a single cylinder motorcycle with a battery fired ignition circuit with points will always have just one set of points and a condenser along with one coil and just one secondary circuit (spark plug lead) going to the spark plug.

A twin cylinder can have two sets of points and condensers and two coils, with one secondary circuit (spark plug lead) coming out of each coil.

A twin cylinder can also have one set of points and condenser and one coil with two secondary circuits (spark plug lead) coming out of the one coil, one to each spark plug.

A three cylinder bike with a battery fired ignition circuit with points, will always have three sets of points and condensers along with three coils with just one secondary circuit (spark plug lead) coming out of each coil, going to each spark plug.

All four cylinder bikes will have two sets of points and condensers, along with two coils with two secondary circuits (spark plug leads) coming out of each coil, leading to each spark plug.

The only thing different between a single cylinder with a battery fired ignition circuit with points, and a multi-cylinder battery fired ignition circuit with points is the number of components.

They all work exactly the same way and they work independent of each other. This means that no matter how many sets of points and condensers you have, they are tested as individual units.

Troubleshooting a Battery-Fired Ignition System With Points

We will troubleshoot a single cylinder bike here. Once you understand how to troubleshoot a single cylinder, you will understand that troubleshooting a multi-cylinder motorcycle is the same, just with more components.

When troubleshooting a battery fired ignition circuit with points, the battery has to be in good condition, properly connected and fully charged. If this isn't the case, the ignition system will not fire, because the power for the ignition circuit comes from the battery.

All the wires for the ignition system must be clean and properly connected.

Ten percent of the time, the reason you have no spark is because you have a blown fuse in the ignition system's wiring circuit, so check the fuses first.

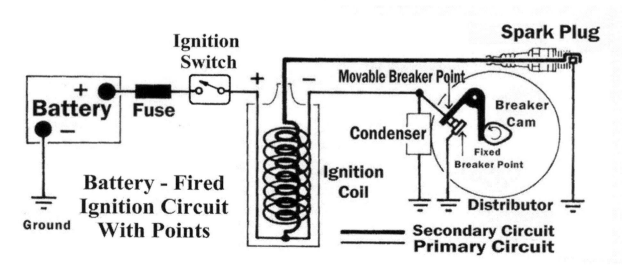

Eighty per cent of the time, if there is a "no spark" condition, or a weak spark condition, with this ignition system, it will be either a bad battery, or it will be the points or condenser that are at fault.

Once you have checked the fuse and it is good, check the battery. Use your service manual as a guide. When in doubt, throw it out and get a new battery, (see Chapter 8 – Battery Charging Systems); especially if you have an electric starter and it won't crank over the bike due to low battery power after it's been charged.

Once you know for sure that you have a good battery and it is fully charged, take a look at the points to see if they're in alignment with each other. Check that the points are not pitted. Pitting is metal that has transferred from one point to another leaving a crater in one of the points and a small mountain of metal on the other point. If you have pitting, it's the condenser fault. Get a new set of points and a new condenser. Install the points and condenser, (check your service manual for instructions on installing the points and condenser).

If your points are good (or after you have replaced your points and condensers), get an electric ice-pick tester (see Chapter 12 on Tools). Use the ice-pick tester to test for electrical current at the points when the ignition switch is on.

First test the tester by grounding the alligator clip to a known good ground (the negative side of the battery if you have a negative grounded battery), then touch the positive side of the battery with the tester tip. A light in the tester should light up, showing that the tester is good and you have current flowing through the tester.

Turn the bikes ignition switch on, and touch the movable breaker point with the testers sharp tip while you are opening and closing the points. (Yes this can be done while cranking the bike over); the light in the tester should flash on and off as the points open and close.

If you don't get a flashing light while the points are open and closing, then (a.) you don't have a good connection to the battery through the coil to the movable breaker point; or (b.) the movable breaker point is grounded or fouled.

Start by disconnecting the coils primary wire to the points. Remove the wire where it mounts to the movable breaker point and use the ice-pick tester to see if you have electrical current to the end of wire.

If you have current to the end of the coils primary circuit where it meets the movable breaker point, then the problem is that the movable breaker point is fouled or grounded to the motor and it shouldn't be. Replace the points and condenser as a set. See your service manual for instructions on replacing your points and condensers.

If you don't have current on the primary circuit that is coming from your coil, trace the positive side of the battery to the fuse. See if you still have current on both sides of the fuse. Using your ice-pick tester, ground the alligator clip while touching the sharp tip of the tester to both sides of the fuse. You should have current on both sides of the fuse. If you don't, find out why.

Next, go to the ignition switch and test it the same way as you did the fuse. You want to see if current is going into the ignition switch and out again when the switch is turned on. If you have current to the switch and don't have current coming out when the ignition switch is on, then the ignition switch is bad; replace the ignition switch.

The coil is next. See if you have current coming from the ignition switch to the coils positive side. If you do, and you don't have current coming out of the coils primary circuit to the points, the coil is bad and needs to be replaced.

Once you have current to the points and the tester flashes when you open and close the points, redo the spark test. If you have spark, then set the spark timing. See your service manual for the details of setting your spark timing.

Once you have done the timing, then check the advance. Once you have spark and timing along with a proper advance, you are finished with troubleshooting this system; go to Chapter 6 on Fuel Systems.

Still no spark? Then if you have not done so, replace the points and condenser with a brand new set, and redo the spark test.

Still no spark? Then test the coil, as your service manual will show you how to do. Replace it if it is not up to specifications and redo the spark test. See Chapter 3 - the 80/20 Rule.

You should have spark. If not, start over at the top of the troubleshooting list and retest all the components as described. The problem is still there? You just haven't found it yet, but you will. When you get your spark up and timed and the advance is working right, then go to Chapter 6 on Fuel Systems.

Timing the Battery-Fired Ignition System With Points

Before you start to time the battery fired ignition system with points, you will have to look in your service manual for the location of the ignition timing marks for your particular motorcycle. All the details for timing your particular motorcycle are in your service manual – we will be sending you to your manual throughout this procedure.

Once you know where the timing marks are, uncover them so you can see them and the points at the same time. If your bike does not have timing marks, then follow the instructions for timing your motorcycle that's in your service manual.

At this point, you should have spark; if not, go to Chapter 3 to troubleshoot your spark system.

You know where your timing marks are and you have spark? Great!

We are going to tell you how to time a single cylinder battery fired points system. If you're doing a double points, or a triple points system, then it is the same, only with more points to set. Each set of points will have their own timing marks.

Read in your service manual how to adjust your points gap and adjust the gap when the points are open all the way. You do this by making sure that the point's cam has opened the points to the points widest position.

Some understanding – the points control when the spark plug fires. It does this when the points open. So you want to control when the points open in order to control the spark timing.

When the points open, the electrical current that has been stored in the ignition coil when the points were closed, is sent to the spark plug where it jumps the air gap making a spark. When the points open on a battery fired system, you will get a spark. It doesn't matter if the points are timed or not, you will get spark every time the points open.

The ignition coil fires when the points open, because the battery is providing the electrical current that powers the coil. The points are just a cam driven switch that controls when the high voltage current leaves the ignition coil. So you have to adjust the points in order to set the timing.

Once you have set the points maximum opening to the specifications in your service manual, you can set the timing.

The points are usually on a moveable plate. This plate can be moved to advance or retard the timing (move the timing forward or backward) depending on what the timing marks tell you.

You will need a timing light. See how to set up a timing light under "Timing Magneto Points Ignition System".

Put the spark jump test tool you have made (see Chapter 12 on Tools) in the spark plug cap that is on the cylinder you are testing. Check to make sure you have spark at the spark test tool.

Once you have the timing light set up, crank the motor over as if you were attempting to start it.

The timing light should flash every time the points open. All you have to do is move the plate that the points are on until the timing marks line up and that set of points are timed.

If the moving timing mark is in front of the stationary timing mark when the timing light flashes, then the timing is too far advanced. Move the points plate until the timing marks line up.

If the moving timing mark is behind the stationary timing mark, then the timing is retarded. Move the points plate so the timing marks line up.

When the timing marks are lined up, lock the screws down that hold the points plate in place.

Find the timing advance mark and do the timing advance check. You will find out how in your service manual.

If your timing does not advance, or it does not advance to the right position as shown in your service manual, then you have a problem with a bad timing advancer. Replace it with a new one. Repeat setting the timing on any other points you have.

Once all the timing is done and the advance is good, then you're through with timing. Move on to Chapter 6 on Fuel Systems.

In a Nut-Shell

When the points open, the system fires a spark to the spark plug.

Overview of the Magneto Points Ignition System

The magneto points ignition system is one of the oldest ignition systems used on motorcycles. It's simple, it's reliable, and it's easy to work on. Let's start with the components, which are few in number.

The magneto has a rotating magnet flywheel (see Chapter 3 – The Rotating Magnet/Coil), that passes by the primary coil. The primary coil's job is to make and send current to the ignition coil but in this case, it can't because the points are closed. When the points are closed, the current goes to ground instead of the ignition coil.

When the point's cam turns, it opens the points at the same time that the rotating magnet is moving past the primary coil. Just as the points open, the primary coil will then shoot a strong surge of electrical current to the ignition coil that then fires the spark plug.

The ignition coil is a stepped-up transformer that converts the current coming from the primary coil to current of a higher voltage. This higher voltage current is capable of jumping the air gap at the spark plug, making a spark.

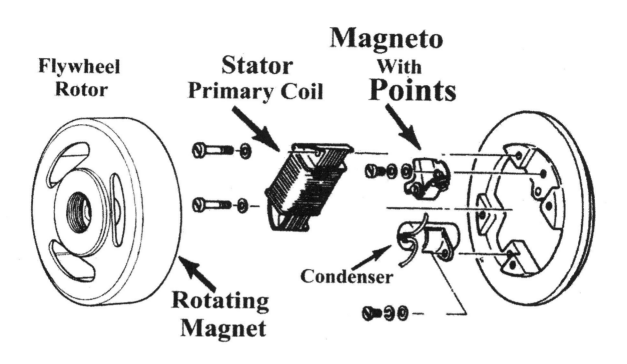

Flywheel Rotor

Stator Primary Coil

Magneto With Points

Rotating Magnet

Condenser

When the spark plug fires, it ignites the compressed fuel/air mixture that has come in through the carburetor. This exploding fuel/air mixture pushes the piston back through the cylinder, changing the chemical energy into mechanical energy. So long as this sequence of events is repeated, the motor runs.

The condenser helps by reducing the arcing at the points. The ignition kill switch grounds the system, killing the spark. The magneto points ignition system must be mechanically timed. This means that the flywheel must be timed to the crank. This is done with a key-way. The key-way is a piece of steel that aligns the flywheel to the crank. If this key-way is not in place or it is broken, the flywheel will be out of alignment.

If the flywheel is out of alignment with the crank, when the points open, the points will be out of time with current coming from the primary coil and there will be no current to send to the ignition coil and no spark.

When the flywheel is timed to the crank and the points open, just as the rotating magnets pass the primary coil, the current will be sent to the ignition coil and there will be spark at the spark plug's air gap.

The points must be timed too. The points must open within a very limited angle of flywheel rotation. On most bikes there are timing marks on the case and on the flywheel. If you don't have timing marks, see your manual on how to adjust your timing. Once the bike has spark, you can use a timing light to time the points.

In a Nut-Shell

The crank and flywheel have to be in alignment and the points have to be properly adjusted to get a timed, hot spark.

Troubleshooting the Magneto Points Ignition System

Now that you understand the magneto points ignition system, let's find out what's wrong with yours.

You have a "no spark" condition, or a "weak spark".

With this system, 80% of the time when you have a weak spark or no spark condition, the fault is in the points or condenser. Start with the easy stuff first.

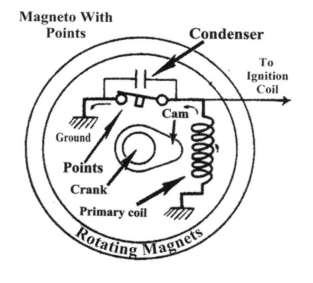

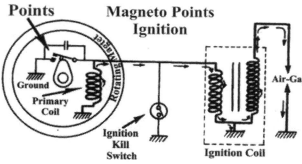

Check your kill switch first to see if it is staying on and shorting out the ignitions system. Remember that on this system, the ignition switch just turns the bike off, not on. Temporarily unplug the kill switch from the system.

Make sure that all the connections are clean and tight and in the right place. See your wiring diagram in your service manual for wiring details. Now re-try the spark test. If you get spark – great! Go to your manual and read the chapter on timing your ignition system.

No spark! The magneto points system is a one-wire system. It goes from the magneto's points to the engine coil. You will need to pull the magneto-flywheel.

You will need the mag-puller that was made for your bike and NO OTHER. Don't mess around here, get the right puller from your motorcycle dealership.

Read how to pull your magneto's flywheel-rotor in your service manual. Pull the magneto's flywheel, and as you do, look for the crank flywheel timing key-way. You will find it between the crank and the flywheel mounting surface. Make sure that it is in place and not broken.

The key-way has to be there and in place, when you re-assemble the magneto. The key-way is what keeps the crank timed to the flywheel. Without the key-way in place, you will not get any spark because the mechanical timing will be out of alignment.

Once the flywheel is off, look at the points to see if they are burned or pitted. If the points are burned or pitted, replace them with a new set of points and condensers. They're not worth messing around with, so just replace them.

Next, look at the primary coil. If there is visual damage, do a resistance test. (See your service manual for the primary coil resistance test specifications). If the primary coil doesn't pass the resistance test, then replace it. See the 80/20 Rule.

Look for frayed wiring. If there is frayed wiring, repair it so that it won't short out the system. Move the points as far away as possible from the center of the magneto and lock it down with the screw. This gives the rotor proper clearance. Then put the flywheel rotor back on, making sure that the key-way is in place. The number one reason that key-ways break is due to not tightening up the flywheel nut enough, so re-torque that nut to where your service manual says it should be.

Re-do the spark test. Do you have spark? Yes! Great! Move on to timing the magneto points system.

Still no spark? If you have not done so, do a resistance test on both the primary coil and the ignition coil. There will be a resistance test in your service manual. If either is bad, then replace it. See the 80/20 Rule.

What, still no spark? Okay – redo all the tests again from the top taking your time because the problem is there somewhere and you will find it. (See Chapter 3 - the 80/20 Rule).

Now you have spark – you found it, good! Now you will need to time the points. Go to your service manual and look up how to time your points for your particular motorcycle engine. We will cover how to adjust the timing, in "Timing Magneto Points", but read how to time your bike in your service manual first.

Timing a Magneto Points Ignition System

Ninety-nine percent of the time, if you have a magneto points system, you have a single cylinder motorcycle. If you have a multi-cylinder motorcycle with a magneto points system, you need to see your service manual for how to time your particular bike.

If your motorcycle does not have timing marks on the magneto's flywheel and on the case, or just inside the flywheel, then you need to see your service manual for the proper way to time your motor.

If you have a magneto points ignition system with two timing marks on the flywheel, then you can use the technique we will describe here to time the spark, but you will have to read your service manual to figure out which mark to time to.

Now, for the other 99% of the magneto points ignition systems out there!

You have a single cylinder motorcycle with a magneto and one set of points and one condenser and a single timing mark on the flywheel and a timing mark on the case or just inside the magneto's flywheel hole. We will call this non-moving timing mark the "stationary timing mark".

You have spark, but it is not timed. If you have not set the timing, then it's not timed. Trust us on that! Or at the very least you don't know if it's timed correctly. Not having the right timing can damage your engine, so let's time it!

You have to have spark in order to be able to time the spark on a magneto points system. There are a lot of things that the manuals will tell you in regard to timing your mag points system, like using a light or a tone generator to set the timing with. But we have not seen any of these work in over 20 years of setting timing on mags, so we will tell you how do it the way we do it.

With the cover off of the magneto so you can see the points, and the spark plug out, position yourself so that you can see the flywheel and the points through the holes. Turn the flywheel with your hand in the same direction as the motor turns when it's running. The points should close and then open as the timing mark on the flywheel just moves past the stationary timing mark.

The goal is to get the points to open just as the two marks line up. If the points are not opening just as the two marks meet, then loosen the points screw and adjust the points so they do and then lock the screw down so the points don't move.

Look at the points again as the flywheel marks meet the stationary timing mark and see if the points just open as the mark on the moving flywheel reaches the stationary mark on the case. You don't need to be right on, but you need to be close to get a hot spark and you will need a hot spark to fire the timing light.

Repeat the adjustment described above until you get the points just opening when the two marks meet and you have a spark that passes the spark jump test (see Chapter 3 – Spark, How to Do a Spark Test.)

Now you may need another person to help you set the timing, because on most bikes with a mag points system, you have a kick lever on the right side and your mag is on the left side of the bike. It's impossible to kick the bike over and watch the timing light at the same time, (unless you are a contortionist), so find someone to push on the kick lever with their hand while you time the motor.

You will need a 12 volt battery because your bike probably doesn't have one, and you need a 12 volt battery to fire the timing light.

Now you will need a 12 volt timing light along with the spark jump test tool you should have made already. If not, go to Chapter 12 – Tools, and make it now.

Great! Now you have what you need. Put the spark jump test tool in the spark plug cap and ground it to the head (top of the motor) so you can see it when it sparks. Crank over the motor, and you should have a spark jump the spark jump test tools air gap.

You need the spark to jump the spark jump test tools air gap or you will not get a flash at the timing light. You will not get a flash at the timing light if the spark does not jump far enough to make the timing light work. That is why we have had you make the spark jump test tool. The spark jump test tool forces the spark to jump a gap long enough to fire the timing light.

Set up the battery and the timing light by putting the timing light pickup coil around the spark plug wire just above the spark plug cap and making sure that it's closed around the spark plug wire. Then put the timing light leads to the battery, positive to positive and negative to negative. Have your helper turn the motor over fast and see if the timing light flashes.

Once the timing light flashes five or six times every time your helper turns the motor over, you're ready to time the motor.

Point the timing light at the stationary timing mark and watch as it flashes. When the timing light flashes, the moving timing mark will seem to freeze in place. Now the question is, is the moving timing mark in front or behind the stationary timing mark?

If the moving timing mark is in front of the stationary mark when the timing light flashes, then the timing is too far advanced and the points need to be closed a little. Move the points a little (very little at a time). The points control the timing and are very sensitive to adjustment, as you will see.

If the moving timing mark is behind the stationary timing mark when the timing light flashes, then the timing is retarded and the points need to be opened a little.

When the moving timing mark is right on the stationary timing mark when the timing light flashes, then the timing is correct.

After you have got the timing mark set, lock down the point's adjustment screw and recheck the timing. Readjust if needed and you're finished with timing. Go to Chapter 6 - on Overview of Fuel Systems.

Did You Know That?

If your bike has two marks on the flywheel, one will be the timing mark and the other will be the timing advance mark. Check your service manual to see which one is the advance mark and make sure that your timing advance is correct.

Chapter 5

Electronic Ignition Systems

Overview of Electronic Ignition

In all of motorcycle history, no other advent has made motorcycles more reliable than the invention of electronic ignitions systems. What was wrong with points?

At best, points needed to be adjusted and timed. At worst, they got burned, pitted, rusted and shorted out, and when driven at high rpm, they would start to float. Floating means that the points would not hold to the shape of the point's cam.

Points were not reliable, unless you took care of them on a regular basis. In one fell swoop, the electronic ignition removed all of these potential problems. The electronic ignition has also replaced the timing advance mechanism as a source of trouble.

The electronic ignition has only one disadvantage; when it goes out, and sometimes they do, replacement parts are expensive. The number one killer of electronic ignition systems is a combination of heat and vibration.

Even today, most manufacturers hide the electronic ignition systems out of sight, which means, out of the air-flow. The motorcycle industry uses different types of electronic ignition systems on different years, makes and models.

Most dirt bikes and duel sports have magneto fired C.D.I. (capacitor discharge ignition) systems, while street bikes usually have a T.P.I. (transistorized pointless ignition) system or a battery fired C.D.I. system.

If you have a "spark" problem, you will need to find out what electronic ignition system that you have and how to troubleshoot it. If your spark is just fine, then don't worry about it, but it's a good idea to at least have an understanding of how your ignition system works.

Overview of the Transistorized Pointless Ignition System (T.P.I.)

The T.P.I. system was a great move ahead for street motorcycles; a maintenance free ignition system that rarely gives it's owner a problem.

The T.P.I. system is sometimes called the electronic ignition system. The only moving part in the system is the magnet-timing rotor that passes by a small coil which sends a small electrical pulse to the brain box. (See Chapter 3 - on The Rotating Magnet/ Coil). This electrical pulse signals the brain box when to fire a current to the ignition coil.

The ignition coil is a stepped-up transformer that raises the voltage sent to it by the T.P.I's brain box to a point where this higher voltage current can jump the air gap at the spark plug. This high voltage spark will ignite the compressed fuel/air mixture that's come into the engine through the carburetor.

The battery powers the T.P.I.'s brain box, making this system a battery fired ignition system. After the batteries current passes through the fuse and the ignition switch, it reaches the T.P.I. brain box.

There usually is no spark timing to adjust and the brain box takes care of the advance of the spark as the engine speeds up and slows down.

This drawing is for a two-cylinder motorcycle with one ignition coil; both spark plugs fire at the same time. The T.P.I. system has been made for singles, twins, triples, four, and six cylinder motorcycles and is one of the most popular and reliable systems used.

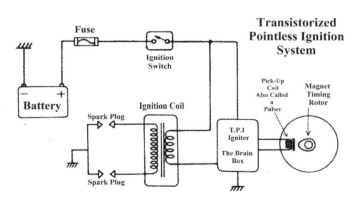

Troubleshooting the Transistorized Pointless Ignition System (T.P.I.)

First, read your service manual under how to troubleshoot your T.P.I. system. Next, check to see that your battery is in good shape and fully charged. The power for the T.P.I. ignition system comes from the battery. If the battery is bad or not fully charged, it will affect this ignition system.

Next, see to it that all the wiring is in the right location and secured. See your wiring diagram in your service manual details. Test the fuse and the ignition switch. Make sure that they both pass current through to the T.P.I.s brain box.

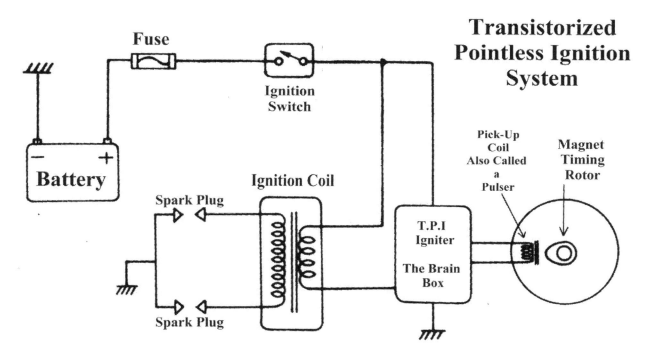

The pulsar coil's job is to send a low powered electrical pulse to the T.P.I.'s igniter/ brain box. If you have spark, the pulse coil is probably okay, but do the resistance tests anyway because if it's not in tolerance it can affect your timing. The resistance test for the pick-up coil can be found in your service manual.

If your pulsar resistance is good and you have no spark or a weak spark, then test the ignition coils resistance. If you have a duel coil system and only have one coil that is firing, you can switch coils and see if the problem follows the coil. If it does, then you have a bad coil. If not, then the trouble is further back in the system, most likely the brain box or the pick-up coil.

If your ignition coil tests good and the pulsar's pick-up coil is testing good, then you have an 80% chance that your T.P.I. igniter/brain box is bad. (See Chapter 3 - the 80/20 Rule). On most bikes, there is no test for the T.P.I. igniter/brain box. On a T.P.I. system, you replace the igniter/brain box only after testing and eliminating all other possibilities.

You should have spark now; if not, re-do all the tests. If all the tests are positive, replace the brainbox.

Once you have spark, test for timing and the timing advance; see your service manual for the details. When you're finished with testing for spark timing and the timing advance, go on to the Chapter 6 on Fuel.

Did You Know That?

Bell Laboratories may have lied when they claimed to have invented the transistor. They may have reverse engineered the technology (appropriated it), from materials taken from the U.F.O. crash at Roswell, New Mexico. Their announcement of this new technology came less than six months after their investigation of the crash.

Overview of Battery-Fired C.D.I. Systems

Read about the T.P.I. system first.

The battery fired C.D.I. system is not as popular with the manufacturers as the T.P.I. system is, but that does not mean it's not a very good system, which it is.

Like the T.P.I. system, the power comes from the battery, and is tested in the same way. The current passes through the fuse and the ignition switch, to what is called the spark unit (brain boxes). A capacitor in the spark unit stores the electrical power that will be sent to the ignition coil. Think of the capacitor as a fast charging-discharging battery.

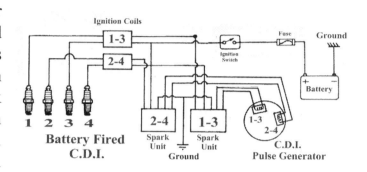

The pulse generator has a rotating magnet that passes the pulsar coil sending a small signal current to the spark unit. (See Chapter 3 - Rotating Magnet Coil). This small current trips the capacitor, which fires a burst of current to the ignition coil.

The ignition coil is a transformer that boosts the voltage so that the higher voltage can jump the air gap at the spark plug. The brain box takes care of the timing and timing advance.

The battery fired C.D.I. is a very reliable system. As with all electronic ignitions systems, 80% of the time the C.D.I. system either works or it doesn't work. This means that it's rare for electronic ignition systems to have a weak spark or an intermittent spark.

Troubleshooting the Battery Fired C.D.I. System

The power for the battery fired C.D.I. system comes from the battery so the battery has to be in good shape and fully charged to produce a good spark.

First, check the battery and the wiring to make sure that all the connections are good and there is a good electrical connection at all connectors.

If you have a "no spark" condition, check the fuse first, then the ignition switch to see that current is passing through them.

Next, go to your service manual and find the troubleshooting page for your C.D.I. system. **Read the troubleshooting layout for your system.** The resistance checks for the C.D.I. pulsar coils (see Chapter 3 - Rotating Magnet Coil) will be there, along with the colour code.

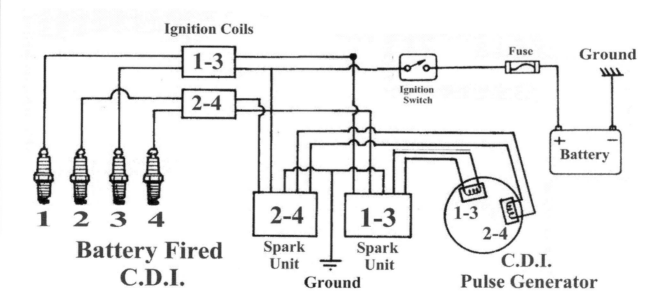

Test the pulsars first; if they're not within the resistance specifications, replace the pulsar's coil. Next, test the ignition coil for resistance. If it's good, great; if not, replace it with a new one.

On most bikes, the spark unit does not have a test. If the pulsar tests "good" and the ignition coil tests "good", then you have an 80% chance that the spark unit is "bad". (See Chapter 3 on the 80/20 Rule). All you can do once you have established that it's not the pulsar or the ignition coil, is replace the spark unit.

Once you get your spark up, check the timing and the timing advance; adjust if it is possible to do so on your bike, then go to Chapter 6 on Fuel Systems.

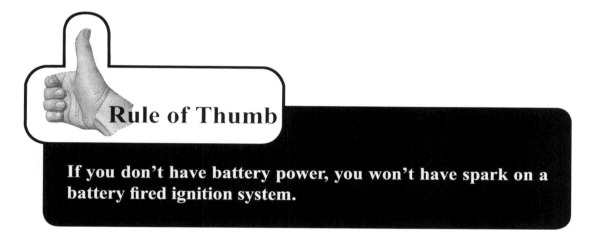

Rule of Thumb

If you don't have battery power, you won't have spark on a battery fired ignition system.

Overview of the Magneto C.D.I. Ignition System

Read about the magneto points ignition system and the battery-fired C.D.I. system first.

The magneto portion of the magneto capacitor discharge ignition system consists of a rotating magnet and two coils; (see Chapter 3 - Rotating Magnet Coil), an exciter coil (primary coil) and a pulsar coil (signal generator).

As the magnet passes by the first coil, (the exciter coil), the exciter coil makes a strong electrical pulse that charges up a capacitor in the C.D.I.'s brain box. The capacitor is an electrical storage unit. This is where the stored current waits until it's told to fire to the ignition coil.

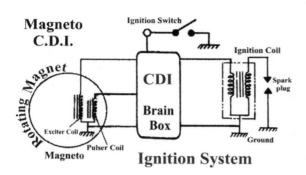

Next, the rotating magnet passes the pulsar coil (signal generator). This sends a small electrical pulse signal to the C.D.I.'s brain box that tells the capacitor to fire it's stored current to the ignition coil.

The ignition coil then transforms the current to a higher voltage that can jump the spark plugs air gap making a spark. This spark then ignites the compressed fuel/air mixture.

Every time the magnet passes the coils, this system just repeats the process.
The ignition coil is a kill switch. It just turns the system off by shorting the C.D.I. to ground.

This system does not have an electrical timing adjustment like the mag-points system does. The timing is pre-engineered into the system. In other words, the timing advance is electronically controlled. However, the rotating magnet flywheel does have to be timed to the crank with a key-way. See Chapter 4, "Overview of Magneto Points Ignition Systems".

The C.D.I. has advantages over the magneto points system. It produces a much hotter spark that reduces spark plug fouling and the C.D.I. system has no points that will burn, pit, or short out. The flywheel is the only moving part and it never wears out.

The C.D.I.'s only disadvantage is that replacement parts don't come cheap. Other than that, it is an almost perfect system.

Troubleshooting the Magneto C.D.I. Ignition System

Read "Overview of the Magneto Fired Ignition System" first.

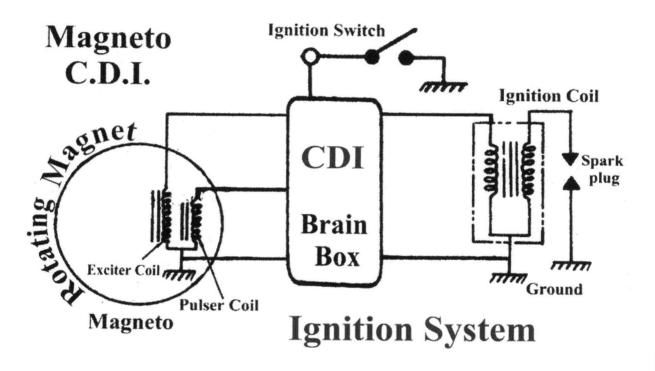

Go to your service manual and find the C.D.I. troubleshooting chapter. Read and understand all that is there.

Most C.D.I. brain boxes cannot be tested directly. You must eliminate all other possibilities, and if you can't find any other possibilities, only then do you replace the C.D.I. brain box.

First, check all the wiring to see if it is connected correctly and that the wiring is secure. Next, check the kill switch to make sure that it's not stuck on, grounding out the system. When in doubt, temporarily disconnect the kill switch from the system. If you have a weak spark, then the pulsar coil is probably okay. It's job is to tell the brain box when to fire, but do the resistance test for the pulsar coil anyway, because if it is not within tolerance, it can affect the timing of the spark. See your service manual for how to do a pulsar resistance test. If it's out of resistance (specifications), replace the pulsar coil. See the 80/20 Rule.

The exciter coil sends the current to the capacitor that is in the brain box. If the exciter coil is bad, it can cause a no spark or weak spark condition. Go to your service manual and find and do the resistance test for the exciter coil. If it's not in tolerance, replace the exciter coil. (See Chapter 3 on the 80/20 rule).

Do you have spark? Great! Then check the spark timing and timing advance; if it's good, move onto Chapter 6 – Fuel Systems).

What, no spark? Okay, then check the ignition coil. You will find the resistance test for it in your service manual. If it's not in tolerance, replace the ignition coil.

No spark still! If you have done all the resistance tests, and they're good, then you have an 80% chance that the problem is your C.D.I.'s brain box.

There is usually no test for the brain box. So, if you have eliminated all the other possibilities by testing, then replace the C.D.I. brain box.

If you still have no spark after replacing the brain box, then you may need to replace some of the parts that test good. (See Chapter 3 on the 80/20 Rule).

You have spark and it jumps the spark jump test tool? Great! Check your timing and timing advance, adjust them; (if it is possible to do so on your bike), and then move on to Chapter 6 – Fuel Systems.

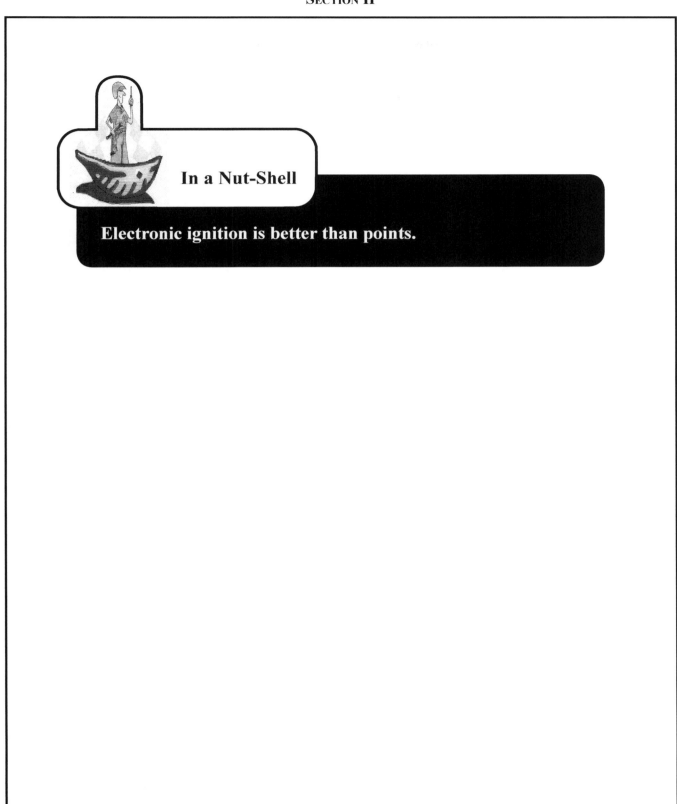

In a Nut-Shell

Electronic ignition is better than points.

Chapter 6

Fuel Systems

Overview of Fuel System

Fuel, gas, it's the same thing!

Gas does not last forever, no matter what the movie "The Road Warrior" says. Gas is good for about 90 days and then it starts going bad. Actually, it's starting to go bad the day it's made, but after 90 days, it starts to affect the way your motorcycle's motor runs. After a year it will smell like turpentine and will not explode in a motorcycle motor.

When in doubt – throw it out! If you don't know how old the gas is, then throw it out and get rid of it and start with new gas.

Don't mess with old gas. Drain your tank and your carburetor(s) BEFORE trying to start your bike.

The first thing we do when a non-running motorcycle comes into our shop is before it's unloaded, we unscrew the gas cap and do a "smell and look" test. We smell the gas to see if it's bad and then look into the fuel tank to see if it's rusted.

The fuel starts at the tank, then it goes through the petcock valve to the fuel lines to a fuel filter (we hope you have a fuel filter on your bike) and then through a fuel pump. If you have a fuel pump, that is. If not, the fuel gravity-feeds to your carburetor (s).

It goes through the carburetor where it's mixed with air at about 15 parts air to one part of gasoline and then it goes into the motor where it is compressed to that minimum pressure of 100 psi. The spark goes off and BANG! You have a fuel/air explosion pushing the piston back through the cylinder.

How much energy does a gallon of gas have?

Run your motorcycle out of gas and then put just one gallon of gas in it and run it at about 10 miles an hour on a flat road until you run out of gas. How far did it go? Let's say you went 50 miles; now push it back to where you started!

Now you have an idea of how much energy is in a gallon of gas.

What kind of gas do we put in our motorcycle? Chevron Unleaded Premium is what we recommend; it's the best and no, they're not paying us to say this either.

A motorcycle engine has only three problems with gas.

1. Old gas; the motor can't burn it.

2. No gas, or too little gas, that makes the bike run lean. This overheats the motor and can cause damage due to over-heating and pre-ignition.

3. Too much gas to air mixture, running rich (runs too cold) and fouls the spark plugs.

Gasoline burns backwards. The more gas to air in the mixture, the cooler the motor runs. Think of your bike as a gasoline-cooled motorcycle. The less gas to air in the mixture, the hotter the motor runs. A motorcycle motor that is not getting enough gas to air mixture will overheat and it can melt down from too much heat.

The number one reason that carburetors need rebuilding is that they have set too long with gas in them without the bike running. Gas has an on-going chemical reaction with your carburetor's parts, and when the lighter portion of the gas evaporates, it leaves behind a varnish type substance that fouls your carbs.

If your motorcycle sets for months at a time, you're building up crud (this is another technical term), due to the chemical reaction and the evaporating fuel in your carburetors. Every time it sets for more than a few weeks, you get more crud built up inside your carbs. After a few years of this, the crud breaks loose and gets sucked up into the jets of your carbs. The jets are the small tubes that let gas through to your motor. The crud blocks the fuel from getting through your jets and your bike starts running hot (lean) or not at all. The answer is to rebuild your carburetors. See (How to Rebuild A Carburetor).

Rust also cruds up the carburetors. Rust comes from your fuel tank and goes into your carbs. This plugs the jets, slowing or stopping the gas from getting through to the motor. Rust can block the float needle valve (the fuel float cut-off valve in the carbs), letting the fuel overflow the float bowl and draining out onto the ground. The answer to the rust problem is to rebuild your carbs, (see How to Rebuild A Carb) and reline your fuel tank. (See How to Re-line a Fuel Tank).

Rule of Thumb

If you drain the carbs and the old gas comes out yellow, you have a 50% chance that they will need rebuilding. If the old gas comes out green, then you have an 80% chance that they will need rebuilding. If rust comes out when you drain your carbs, you have a 99% chance that they will need to be rebuilt and a 100% chance that your fuel tank will need to be relined.

EPA Lean

The Environmental Protection Agency (EPA) in the United States has since the late 1970's, forced the motorcycle industry to make newer motorcycles run leaner and leaner (hotter and hotter) every year.

This over-lean problem is to the point that some brand new motorcycles can't pull away from a stop without over-revving the motor and slipping the clutch a lot more than what is normal. This constant over-heating of the motorcycle's engine is so hard on them, that they will not last as long as they should.

If you take the air filter out of some of these bikes, the bike will not start at all, even with the choke on. This is because the air filter restricts airflow making the motorcycle run a bit richer.

The answer to EPA lean problems is what I call a very "aggressive" cleaning of the carburetor jets. What we mean by "aggressive cleaning" is to drill out the carburetor jets one or two drill bit sizes, this will increase the fuel flow making the carburetor run a bit richer. See Chapter 11, Land of Experimentation.

In a Nut-Shell

The E.P.A. is not your friend when it comes to having your motorcycle run right.

Troubleshooting the Fuel System

You start with the fuel tank. Do a "look and smell" test. If there is rust in the tank then you need to dump the gas out and reline the tank. (See How to Reline A Fuel Tank). No rust? Great. Reline your tank anyway, so you don't get rust in it in the future.

Does the gas smell bad like turpentine? If it does, dump it out. If you don't know if it's bad or not, throw it out (when in doubt – throw it out), especially if it over 90 days old. It's not worth the time or effort to mess with old gas.

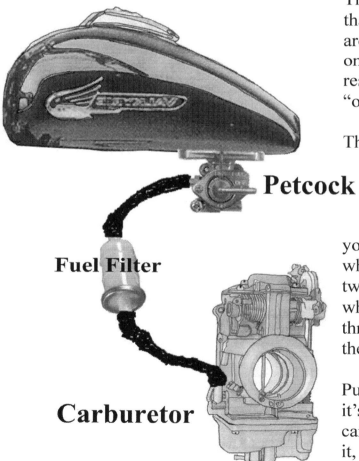

Petcock

Fuel Filter

Carburetor

The petcock is next. That is the valve that turns the fuel on and off. There are basically two kinds of petcocks; one is an on/off type and may have a reserve. It will have three positions, "on", "off", and "reserve".

The other type of petcock is a vacuum petcock. It also has three positions; "on", which is only on when there is a vacuum from the engine. There is a vacuum from the engine when you are trying to start the motor and when the motor is running. Position two is the reserve, but again only "on" when there is a vacuum, and position three is a prime. Prime is "on" whether there is a vacuum or not.

Pull the petcock off and make sure that it's clear and there is no crud in it. You can do this by blowing air through it, and check all the positions for air flow.

If the fuel lines are hard or cracked, and or leaking, take them off and replace them with new lines and clamps. We use zip ties for clamps.

Drain the carbs. There is a drain on the bottom of every carburetor. Open it and see what comes out. If it is yellow gas, you have a 20% chance that you will need to rebuild your carbs. It it's green, you have an 80% chance you will need to rebuild your carbs. If no gas comes out, then someone has drained the carbs of all the gas, or it has evaporated from setting so long.

Look at the drain plug. Does it have crud on it, or is it clean? If it's covered with crud, then you may need to rebuild your carbs. Clean the drain screws, replace and tighten them.

Check your oil level, making sure it is up to the full position.

Take a teaspoon of gas and put it down each spark plug hole, add new spark plugs and new spark plug caps. Now try to start the motor using just the gas you put down the spark plug holes. It should start and run until it runs out of the gas you put in. Great - it started then died.

Now, run gas to your carbs. Do they leak? If they do, then they will need to be rebuilt. (See How to Rebuild a Carburetor).

They don't leak or you have just rebuilt them.

The moment of truth. Put gas to your carbs. Now you have at least 100 psi of compression and you have a hot timed spark. Great! Try starting your motorcycle.

This is the procedure to start your motorcycle every time.

Turn the ignition switch on and try starting the bike WITHOUT USING THE CHOKE.

Give it a good chance to start. If it doesn't start, then bring the choke on slowly until it starts running and then turn the choke off immediately. Don't leave the choke on to warm up the bike; leaving the choke on will foul the spark plugs. Hold the rpm up with the throttle until the bike can idle on it's own.

The bike doesn't start?

Okay, you have compression of at least 100 psi, and a tested hot timed spark. When you put gas down the spark plug hole and installed a new spark plug and a new spark plug cap, it started, ran and died? Yes? Then your carbs need rebuilding because you are not getting enough gas through your carbs.

Another indicator that your carbs need rebuilding is the motor will run with the choke on, but when you turn the choke off, the motor will die or runs badly. (See How to Rebuild A Carburetor).

Your bike starts and runs and sounds good? Great! I KNEW YOU COULD DO IT!!! Now, go to Chapter 10 for Motorcycle Safety Check and Tune & Service.

Overview on Carburetor Rebuild

Read all there is to know about your carbs in your service manual.

Don't freak out, carburetors are not that tough; actually motorcycle carbs are easy once you get to know them. And once again, you only need to learn about the ones on your bike, not every carburetor on every bike.

Some people will rebuild their engine and transmission but be so afraid of the carburetors that they bring them to us to rebuild; it makes no sense. If you can learn to wash the dishes, you can learn to rebuild your carbs.

If you have a multiple cylinder motorcycle, you will usually have a carburetor for each cylinder. The carburetors are identical; they're just repeated for each cylinder, so once you learn how to rebuild one, you can rebuild them all.

There are only three types of carburetors used on motorcycles:

Butterfly, also called a Fixed Venturi carburetor

Pull slide carburetor

Constant velocity, also called a constant depressing carburetor

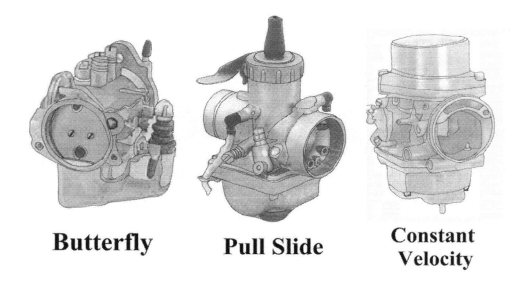

Butterfly   **Pull Slide**   **Constant Velocity**

The butterfly carburetor is used on older motorcycles. They have a butterfly valve that opens when you open the throttle. These carbs are very on/off, meaning that when you open the throttle, the motorcycle gets a big hit of fuel making the bike jump forward. When you shut the throttle down, you get a lot of stopping power from engine drag. As a result, with butterfly carbs, you get a lot of jerkiness.

Pull slides have a slide that goes up when you twist the throttle. They're on almost all dirt bikes and the older street bikes. They're a better (in our opinion) carburetor, than the butterfly and not quite as jerky.

Constant velocity carburetors are pull-slides that have a diaphragm connected to the top of the slide. They are pulled up by vacuum from the motor and pushed back down by a spring. CV carbs are smoother because they use the vacuum from the motor to control the carbs.

C.V. are used on almost all modern street bikes. Most motorcycles have only one carb per cylinder; if you have a four-cylinder bike, you probably have a bank of four carbs.

Some single cylinders have two carbs; one for the low rpm and one for the high rpm.

Some twin cylinders have just one carb for both cylinders.

Some four cylinder bikes have just two carburetors. Some six cylinder bikes have six carbs, and some have three two-barrel carbs.

As you can see, every bike can be different on the carb layout, but the carbs all do the same thing. They meter the gas into an air-stream so your bike gets the fuel/air mixture it needs no matter what rpm the motor is at.

Carburetors are like a toilet. They have a float bowl and a float that lets the fuel go only so high, then cuts the fuel off so it can't overflow the carb. The valve that does this is called the float needle and seat.

Every carb has jets. Jets are just a fancy name for tubing with a very precise hole that sticks down into the gas in the float bowl. These jets let the gas move into the throat of the carb when there is vacuum from the engine.

Every motorcycle service manual has an expansion view of how your particular carbs work. Your service manual will also tell you how to R & R (remove and re-install) and how to rebuild them. Read your manual and become the expert on your carbs.

Remember that you do not have to design the carbs; that was done for you at the factory. All you have to do is pull them off the bike and take them apart and clean them and replace any bad parts, then reassemble them and put them back on the bike. All the information for you on how to do this, is in your service manual.

Your service manual will give you a step by step list of how to take your carbs off of your bike and how to rebuild them and put them back on. Take your time and remember if you do not do it right the first time, you get another chance. You can do it again. Also, if you want to know more than what is in your service manual, there is a whole book just on motorcycle carburetors called "The Motorcycle Carburetor Manual" by Pete Shoemark.

How to Rebuild a Carburetor

Once you know that the carbs are the problem, it's time to rebuild them. (If you have rust in your fuel tank, see "How to Re-line Your Fuel Tank".

If you do not have rust, you can do a flush of the carbs. This is a trade secret. You do this on bikes that start and run, but run rough, due to fouled carbs.

Drain the carbs and fill them with a special cleaner we stole from the marine industry. It's called "Power Tune Engine Cleaner" and is available at any Mercury dealer or boat motor repair shop.

Fill the carbs through the fuel line. This engine cleaner is the best damned carb cleaner that you can get and it will desolve the crud. By doing a carb flush, 30% of the time, you will not have to go to the trouble of removing and rebuilding the carbs.

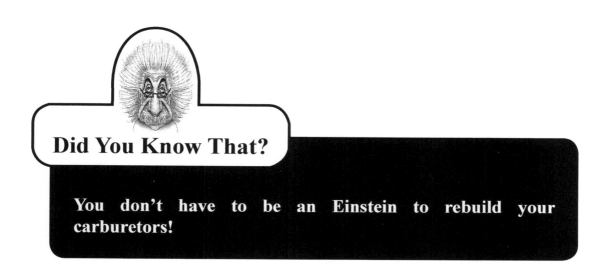

Did You Know That?

You don't have to be an Einstein to rebuild your carburetors!

How to Flush Your Carburetors

Drain all the gas out of the carbs.

Fill the carbs with engine cleaner; the engine cleaner comes in a spray can with a big plastic tip that you can put into the fuel line.

Keep filling until the carbs overflow. Wait a few minutes and then fill them again. The engine cleaner is very foamy and it may take several times of spraying until it really fills the carbs to overflowing.

Once they're filled, let the carbs set overnight and then drain them the next day. Refill the carbs with new Power Tune Engine Cleaner and let them set overnight again.

The next day, turn the bike over as if you were trying to start it. This lets the engine cleaner go through the jets into the engine and helps to clean the jets.

Then open the drain plugs in the bottom of the carbs and drain all the engine cleaner out. Add fresh gas and start up the bike and see how it runs. If it is better, but not great, then repeat the flush process until it gets to the point where the carbs will not improve with flushing.

At this point, make a decision. Can you live with the carbs the way they are, or do you need to rebuild them? If your choice is to rebuild them, then using the engine cleaner has helped to pre-clean the inside of the carbs.

Rebuilding Your Carburetors

In this section, we describe the method used for rebuilding a single carburetor. If you have multiple carbs, just duplicate this process for each carburetor.

Pull the tank, side covers and seat if needed.

Loosen the rear carb clamp and remove the screws that hold your air box in place and pull the air box away from the carbs as far as possible; on some models you can remove it.

There's a clamp that holds the carburetor onto the motor; loosen this clamp and pull the carb back and to the side and then take off the throttle and choke cables and remove the carb from the bike. Compared to rebuilding the carbs, the hard part is getting the carbs on and off the bike.

Clean the outside of the carb with a toothbrush and engine degreaser before taking the carb apart. You do this so the crud on the outside of the carb doesn't get into the carb.

Leave multiple carbs all mounted together. Do not take multiple carbs off their mounts without a very good reason.

Check all the outside mechanical parts to see if they're working correctly.

Next, take the float bowls off, making sure you know where all the parts go, so you can put them back correctly. If you have more than one carb, you can always look at the other carb to see how the first one goes back together.

Start cleaning the float bowls by scraping all the crud out.

After the crud is out, put Mercury Power Tune Engine Cleaner into the float bowls and let it set.

Then start pulling the float needles and seats out.

Remove the idle enrichness screw, if it has one. The idle enrichness screw may be covered with an E.P.A. plug that may need to be drilled and pulled; if so drill it and pull the plug. Be careful with your drilling, because the screw is right under the plug.

Pull all the removable jets and clean out all the holes in the carb body by blowing air through them.

Make sure that the passage between the pilot jet and the idle enrichness screw is clear. Do this by putting some WD-40 down the pilot jet hole and blow air through the pilot hole, so you can see the WD-40 coming out the idle enrichness screw hole.

Do not take off the top of the carbs unless you have a good reason. If they're working, leave them alone.

After all the jets are clean and the inside of the carb is clean, inspect all the parts for wear and damage. Replace all the damaged and worn parts with new ones. Many times carbs don't need parts, they just need a good cleaning.

If the jets are blocked so that you can't see through them, find an old throttle cable and cut off about three inches. Pull out the wires that are inside and find the one in the middle and unravel it. You will find that at the center there is just one straight wire. Use this wire to clean out the small jets. This is a trade secret.

A motorcycle repair shop should give you an old throttle cable or, if you can't find an old throttle cable, then try using a torch tip cleaner from a welders supply shop. If all else fails, buy new jets of the right size from the dealership that sells your brand of motorcycle.

Once the jets are clean and/or replaced, reassemble the inside of the carburetors.

Look the float height up in your service manual and set the float height as described, then put the float bowl back on.

Set your fuel enrichness screw per your service manuals specifications.

Lubricate all the external parts with WD-40.

Next, test the carb to make sure it doesn't leak. Put gas to the carb through the fuel line to the point that you're sure that the carb is full, plus some. The goal here is to make sure that the carb doesn't leak before you go to the trouble of putting it back on the bike.

You can run a fuel line from the tank to the carb without mounting the carb to the bike. Once the carb is filled, tilt it slowly side to side and front to back. You should get to about 45 degrees of movement before it starts to overflow. If so, it's good. Remount the carb onto the bike.

Replacing the carb on the bike is a reversal of taking it off.

Make sure you put a brand new in-line fuel filter on your motorcycle; it's good insurance against having to do another carb rebuild.

Last, but not least, if there is more than one carb on your bike, you will need to synchronize the carburetors. See Chapter 10 on "Tune and Service" and "Setting & Synchronizing Carburetors".

Note, that you did not pull the top off of the carb, and you did not take the multiple carbs off of their mounts. They stayed together unless you had a very good reason to pull them apart.

Do not put a rebuilt carburetor back on a motorcycle that has rust in the tank. The rust will just run through the fuel line and crud up your carbs again. If you have rust, see "How to Re-line Your Fuel Tank".

Rebuilding your carbs usually takes care of all the carburetor problems; if not, then see Chapter 11 - The Land of Experimentation.

Overview of Relining a Fuel Tank

When you have rust in your gas tank, you need to get it out or else the rust will clog up your carburetors if it hasn't already done so. You will also need to reline the inside of the tank with a product called Kreem.

Before using this product, read all of the instructions that come with the relining kit. If you have a lot of rust, you will need to pre-gravel your fuel tank prior to using the Kreem kit. If you have a small amount of rust spotting, you can just use the Kreem kit without pre-graveling the tank.

A fuel filter will just stop the big chunks of rust, but the small dust size particles will go right through most fuel filters, clogging the jets that are inside your carburetor and making a carb rebuild necessary.

Pre-graveling is adding gravel, soap and water to the inside of the tank and then shaking the tank so the gravel etches the rust out. After all the rust is out, then you start the relining process.

How to Reline a Fuel Tank

You can get a Kreem re-lining kit from a motorcycle dealership.

Read all the instructions in the Kreem package and understand them before starting.

There is rust in your tank. The question is, is it just some small rust spots or is it a lot of rust?

If it is just a few spots, you can use the Kreem tank liner kit without graveling the fuel tank. If the inside of your fuel tank is covered with rust, then you will have to gravel it first.

Graveling a fuel tank is done when you remove the petcock and the fuel sensor float (if it has one), and cover up the holes. Next, you put an abrasive in the tank. We use about five pounds of gravel.

After you add the gravel to the tank, add water (about 1/2 a gallon) and some dish soap. Now it's time to go to work. It's cocktail shaker time. You have to shake the tank so that the gravel rubs the inside of the tank enough to scrape the rust off. This takes time so don't be in a hurry.

When you're ready, pour the water out; you will see rust in the water. Now, add new water and soap and re-shake the tank and continue pouring the water out again and again adding more soap and fresh water as you go.

Repeat this process until no rust comes out with the water. Then, using a flashlight if needed, look inside the tank. If there is no rust left, dump all the gravel out of the tank. Now you're ready to start the re-lining process.

Follow the instructions that come with the three-part kit of Kreem tank liner.

What You Need to Know About Motorcycle Tank Relining

The Kreem tank re-liner's chemicals should not come into contact with you or your motorcycle tanks paint.

The white Kreem liner will stop up any holes, including the bolt holes that hold your petcock and the fuel float sensor on, so put grease on the bolts and put them in place prior to using the white liner. If you don't, your bolts will not go back in.

Your fuel cap should be removed from the tank while doing the white Kreem re-lining part. Use duct tape for a cap instead.

It says in the instructions not to use a hair dryer, but we have had great success using a low temperature bonnet hair dryer. A bonnet hair dryer has a lot less heat than the hand-held type of hair dryer. When it's time for the tank to dry, we pull off the bonnet and stick the hose right in the tank and leave it running on the "cool" heat setting overnight.

When you're done, the tank will have a nice white lining that is impervious to gas and rust, and it will last for the life of the motorcycle.

If you do not have rust in your tank then you do not need to gravel the tank.

Go directly to using the Kreem 3 part reliner kit.

How to Reline Your Fuel Tank

• Remove the fuel tank from the motorcycle and drain the fuel out.

• Remove the petcock, (the fuel valve).

• Remove the fuel sensors float, if it has one.

• Pull the gas cap off.

• Plug or tape up the holes that are in the bottom of the tank.

• Add the gravel, water and soap to the inside of the tank.

• Start shaking the tank so the gravel scrapes the rust off all the interior walls of the fuel tank.

• Pour the water out and replace the water with fresh water.

• Repeat until no more rust comes out with the water.

• Shake the gravel out of the tank and replace the plugs or tape that sealed the holes in the bottom of your fuel tank with new plugs or tape.

Note:
If you have little or no rust in your fuel tank, start the relining process here.

Using the Kreem 3 Part Reliner Kit

Start by using the 3 part Kreem kit by adding Part A and water to the tank. Part A is an acid that will finish etching the inside of the tank. Leave part A in the tank overnight.

Drain out part A and immediately add Part B. Part B is a high evaporant. It's job is to get the water out of the tank and to dry the tank. Rotate the tank to get part B up and all over the inside of the tank and then dump it out.

When the tank is dry, replace the tank plugs, with new clean plugs and grease all the screws and put them back in place. Greasing the screws keeps them from being frozen in place by the white reliner.

Add half of the white Kreem tank liner to the inside of the tank and cover the gas cap hole with duct tape.

Rotate the fuel tank completely. The goal here is to get the white tank liner up on all the inside walls of the tank evenly, with as many layers as possible.

Once the whole inside is covered with white liner, open up the gas cap cover and let the tank set for an hour, and then repeat the relining process by again rotating the tank and letting it set again. Repeat this process until all the Kreem tank liner is sticking evenly to the inside in multiple layers.

Once all the liner is up on the inside of the tank, then let the tank set until it is tacky to the touch. Then add the rest of the tank liner to the tank and start over again with the lining process. Repeat until all the liner is up on the inside walls and the inside top of the tank.

At this point, you can just let the tank set until it dries or you can use a bonnet hair dryer to speed up the process.

Make sure that you have plenty of ventilation, because the gases that come off during the drying process are not good to breathe.

When the tank is fully dry inside, take out the plugs and reassemble the tank making sure that you install a new petcock gasket, and you're finished.

In a Nut-Shell

When you reline your fuel tank this way, it will last for the lifetime of your motorcycle.

Chapter 7

Things That Go Bad From Setting & How to Fix Them

The Battery

The battery loses about 1% of its energy per day, and after 50 days of not being used or charged, the battery starts to die. In 100 days, it's flat and after one year it's no longer savable. If the battery still has some power left, try charging it overnight. It may come up, but if not, then get a new battery. We suggest Interstate Batteries, because they have one of the best warranties.

The Fuel

The fuel starts going bad as soon as it is made, and 90 days after you buy it, the gas will start to have a negative effect on how your motorcycle runs. In the gas tank, gas just gets old and starts to smell like turpentine, but in the carburetors, the gas reacts with the interior of the carbs. This results in crud (a technical term) building up, that fouls the jets in the carbs. Dump out the old gas, reline the fuel tank, rebuild the carbs (if needed), and put some new fuel lines on along with a new fuel filter.

Petcock

Fuel Filter

Carburetor

Brakes

In hydraulic brake systems:

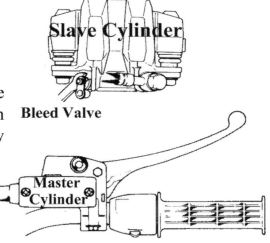

Bleed Valve

The pistons in the master cylinder and in the slave cylinders (calipers), corrode and rust from prolonged setting. They need replacing if they lockup and will not release when you let go of the brake lever. Make sure that you use the right brake fluid when you bleed your brakes. If the slave cylinders, (the calipers), are frozen from lack of use and will not move, then replace them.

Shoe Brakes

Shoe brakes also corrode and they can fall apart; replacing the brake shoes will take care of the problem.

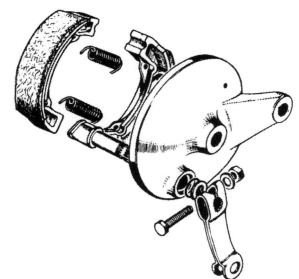

Electrical

Electrical terminal connectors corrode and need cleaning so that they can carry the current without undue resistance. Use electrical contact cleaner and an old toothbrush.

Did You Know That?

A batteries current travels from the negative pole to the positive pole. Sorry about that Benjamin Franklin, it was a good guess on your part, but you were wrong.

The Points

The points also corrode from setting and may need to be cleaned and/or replaced along with the condenser.

Pitted Points & Condenser

Switches

Switches will freeze up from setting. They usually need replacing when they get this bad.

Light Bulbs

We have seen light bulbs rusted in place, frozen in their sockets from setting too long. Most of the time, you have to replace the socket and the bulb.

Bearings

The grease that is in the bearings can dry up and not give good lubrication; replacing the grease will do wonders to stop wear and tear.

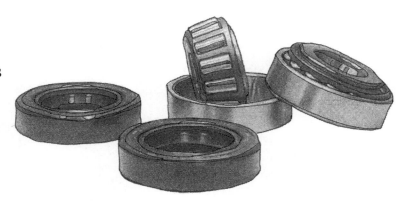

Seals

Seals start leaking just from setting because they shrink and get hard from non-use. Replacement is the only answer.

The Rings

The engine rings are made of chrome molley, or cast iron. The pistons are made of aluminum, the cylinder walls are made of steel; this sets up the process called electrolysis.

Electrolysis means that the electrons are swapping back and forth as in a battery. The electrons can weld the piston rings to the piston and to the cylinder wall so tightly that the engine will not turn over. When this occurs, disassembly and rebuilding the engine is the only answer. Letting the bike set for years without turning the motor over causes this. Starting the motor every month will slow down the electrolysis damage and keep the rings from locking up.

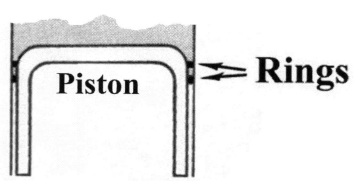

If you have a frozen motor that was running fine before it was left setting, then we suggest that you start by pulling the spark plug and putting a good penetrating oil like WD-40 or Rust Buster down the spark plug hole. Even better, use "Power Tune Engine Cleaner" from a Mercury Marine outlet. Just spray it down the spark plug hole and let it set for a week.

Then try putting the motorcycle in high gear and rocking it back and forth to break the rings loose. Give it time and work it. If the motor does not break loose, then you may want to rebuild it or replace it with a good motor (which is sometimes more cost efficient). If you get the rings loose, then do the make-run procedure.

Rule of Thumb

Prolonged setting without being used, is the number one killer of motorcycles!

Clutch Lockup

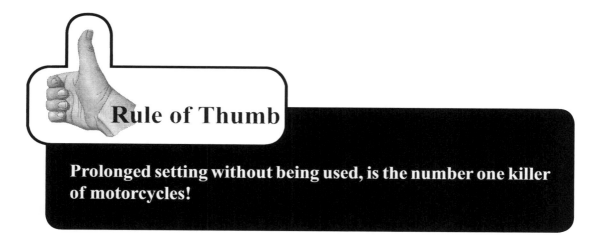

When a motorcycle sets for a long time, the clutch can lock up and not release when you pull the lever in. The lever may feel normal, but the clutch plates are stuck together. Get the motorcycle up and running, and then with the bike running in neutral, tie the clutch lever down.

Push the bike and after it's rolling, shift it into first gear, then ride it until the clutch lets go. You will know when this happens because you will not have power to the rear wheel, because the clutch lever is still tied down. Untie the lever and ride the bike as usual. Yes, you can shift without the clutch on most bikes. Just drop the rpm's and shift up or down.

By using this technique, we get the clutch unstuck 80% of the time. If the clutch does not come unstuck after a few hours of riding, then pull the clutch apart to free the plates.

Tires

Tires go flat from setting – add air. If your tires have gotten hard and developed hairline cracks, we suggest that you get new tires and tubes. You're risking your life riding on bad tires.

Cables

Corrosion can cause a cable to lock up or drag. Taking the cables off of the motorcycle and lubing them with a good lubricant can save a good cable that is sticking, but if the cable is frozen up, replacing it is the best option.

Rubber Things

Anything made of rubber or plastic will get harder with age especially when they're just setting all the time. Rubber and plastic also shrinks with age, and setting just speeds this process up.

In a Nut-Shell

Mother Nature will let you keep your bike, as long as you keep using it.

Chapter 8

Battery Charging Systems

The Battery

What is the heart of the motorcycle? If you have a battery fired ignition system, yes, you've got it, it is your battery.

Without a good battery, your motorcycle will not start and run. If you have an electrical problem, where do you start to search it down? Yes, you start with the battery.

The battery's job is two-fold. One is to store electrical energy and second is to act as an electrical shock absorber for your electrical system. The battery takes the extra electricity that is made by your charging system and turns it into chemical energy. Then when your electrical system needs more current, the battery changes the chemical energy back into electrical current, as needed.

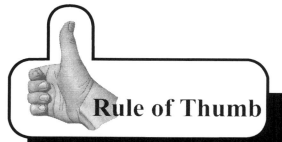

Rule of Thumb

Accidentally reversing the batteries positive and negative terminals, can damage both the charging system and the ignition system on your motorcycle.

When you have a small current surge, the battery absorbs it and this helps to protect your electrical system from damage. For every day that your battery just sets, not being used, it loses about 1% of it's energy. After 50 days of setting, it starts to be damaged and after one year of setting, it is damaged to the point where it will never be as good as it was new.

Some people buy a new battery every year for their bike. Other people use the same battery for five years or more. What is the difference? The people that keep their batteries for years take care of the batteries and the people that purchase a new battery every year don't. It's as simple as that.

Some top of the line motorcycle batteries sell for over $150.00, yours is probably less, but why pay that every year when you don't have to?

The number one reason a battery dies an early death is lack of use, not lack of maintenance. Some batteries are virtually maintenance free and they still die an early death if they're not used on a regular basis.

Because he rides his motorcycle every week, one of our customers is still using the same battery we sold him over ten years ago. Other customers come back every spring to buy a new battery from us. We sell them the battery and then we say, "Do you want to buy a new battery next year, or use this one for years to come?" They always say "Yes, I want to use this battery for years." Then we tell them what we are going to tell you.

Battery Maintenance

The secret to keeping your battery alive, is running your bike between 2,000 and 3,000 rpm at least twice a month for 15 minutes; in other words ride the bike. Simple, isn't it? But most people don't know to do this, or life gets in the way, and they just forget about their bike until the spring.

If this seems to be too much trouble for you, or you're going to be leaving your motorcycle for an extended period of time, then you can use our second technique.

Store the battery on a trickle charger that gives just enough current to the battery only when the battery tells the charger that it needs it. When the battery is in your bike, you should service it once a month by checking the fluid levels and making sure that the battery terminals are cleaned and the battery is fully charged.

That is all you have to do to save money and keep your battery from dying a premature death.

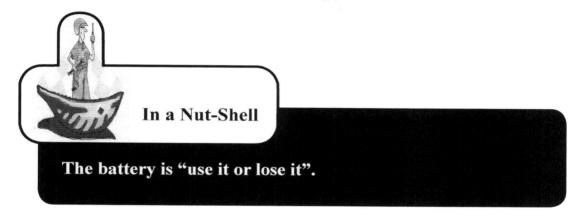

In a Nut-Shell

The battery is "use it or lose it".

Overview of Battery Charging System

If your motorcycle has a battery-fired ignition system, then you will need to have a working charging system so the motorcycle battery can stay charged. If your charging system is not working, then your bike will run until the battery goes dead, at which point the motorcycle will stop running.

If you have a magneto-fired system with a battery, then you do not need a battery for the bike to run, but you will need to charge the battery for the lighting system to continue to work at low rpm.

There is only one charging system on a motorcycle. That charging system is a magnet/coil system. There are only two kinds of magnet/coil charging systems used on motorcycles. The first one is a single phase/half phase system (magneto-type) used for six volt batteries. The second one is a three phase alternating system; its used on all motorcycles with twelve-volt batteries.

The Single Phase/Half Phase (Magneto) System

Read all about your charging system in your service manual.

The single-phase system has moving magnets that pass by a coil of wire that is wrapped around a laminated steel core. When a magnet passes by a coil, it produces AC (alternating current) flow. (See Chapter 3 on The Rotating Magnet Coil).

Alternating current (AC) has both a positive and a negative current flow, and an alternator is constantly switching between the two. This AC current flow is converted to DC and used to charge a DC battery. This is done by placing a rectifier (diode), which is just a fancy name for a one-way gate, in the wire that is leading to the batteries positive side.

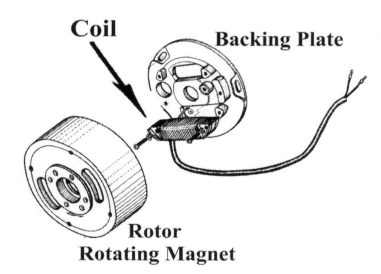

Coil **Backing Plate**

Rotor
Rotating Magnet

This one-way gate lets the positive part of the AC current pass to the positive side of the battery and keeps the negative side out. In order to keep it simple (less expensive), the negative side of the AC current is wasted.

This turns the single phase alternating system into a pulsating half phase DC system that is capable of charging a DC battery. Sometimes this system is designed to have a voltage regulator and sometimes it doesn't; this will depend on the year, make and model of the bike. This half phase pulsating DC system is used for charging six-volt batteries.

The Three Phase Alternating Charging System

Read about how the single phase/half phase system works first (see above), and also read about your charging system in your service manual.

If you have a motorcycle with an electric starter, and a 12 volt battery, you will have a three phase, alternating charging system to charge the battery.

An alternator is three single phase systems wired together in a way that gives a larger, smoother (non-pulsating) output of current; this wiring system is called a stator.

Stator

The stators alternating three phase current passes through a bridge rectifier. A bridge rectifier is a fancy name for a bunch of one-way gates that changed all the current to DC, not just half, like the less expensive half phase system.

Rotor

A motorcycle with a three-phase alternator will also have a voltage regulator to control peak voltage. Controlling peak voltage protects the wiring and its components from overheating and failure.

Did You Know That?

There are two kinds of magnetic rotors for the 12 volt, three phase alternator system. One is an electromagnetic rotor that uses current from the voltage regulator to control the output charging current to the battery. If this system is suspected of not working properly, the electromagnetic rotor can be tested, using a resistance test. You can find this resistance test in your service manual.

The other rotor is a permanent magnet rotor. There is no electrical test for the permanent magnet rotor. After testing and eliminating all other charging system components and finding them good, the only solution for this rotor is to replace it with a good known rotor.

Troubleshooting the Single Phase/Half Phase Magneto Battery Charging System

You must have a good battery that is fully charged before testing this charging system.

First, confirm that you have a charging system problem by doing a battery voltage test. A battery voltage test is done with a voltage meter.

Hook the voltage meter up across the battery with the bike running at 2,000 to 3,000 rpm. If you have a 6 volt battery, your charging system should be putting out 7.5 volts. See your service manual; it will have a charging system troubleshooting guide. Read it and understand how to use it.

You can only truly test the rotating magnets by replacement, and as a last resort. The charging coil can be tested with a resistance test using an ohmmeter; see your service manual for the details for your particular motorcycle. You also need to read Chapter 3 on the 80/20 Rule.

The rectifier can be checked with an ohmmeter also. See your service manual for details of doing the test on your bike.

If you are over-charging, and boiling the battery dry, then you have a bad voltage regulator. Replace the regulator. Replace all the bad components with known good parts, and re-do the voltage out-put test.

Some older single cylinder motorcycles had a system without a voltage regulator. These bikes had a tendency to blow head and taillights. One answer to stopping this from happening, was to add more lighting to use up the excess current.

Troubleshooting the Three Phase Alternator Charging System

Read "Troubleshooting the Single Phase/Half Phase Magneto Battery Charging System" first.

You must have a good battery that is fully charged before testing this charging system.

Do a voltage output check to determine if you really have a charging system problem. Put a voltmeter across your battery. With a 12 volt charging system, you should get 14 to 15 volts at 2,000 to 3,000 rpm; if not, then you have a charging system problem.

If you're over 15.5 volts, then you may have a bad voltage regulator, especially if you are boiling the battery dry or blowing electrical components. See your service manual; it will have a charging system trouble-shooting guide.

Make sure that all electrical wires have a good clean connection. The stator should have three wires coming out of it; most of the time, these three wires are all the same colour. Unplug the stator's electrical terminal connectors from the rest of the bike and do a continuity test. The three wires should have continuity between them with no connection to ground.

If you have continuity to ground, then the stator is shorted out and needs replacement. See your service manual for stator test details. Some alternator rotors have an electrical resistance test. The details for this test is in your service manual.

The rectifier can be tested for proper resistance with an ohmmeter. The rectifier should have continuity in one direction and not in the other. See your service manual for the wiring colour code and details for doing this test.

These components are not fixable, so replacement is the only option when they're found to be bad. After replacing a component, redo the battery voltage out-put test. See Chapter 3 on the 80/20 Rule.

If you want to know more than what's in your service manual, there is a whole book dedicated to just motorcycle electrical systems. The name of this manual is "Motorcycle Electrical Manual" by A. Tranter and yes, you can get it through the Inter-library Loan system at no charge.

Did You Know That?

Six volt batteries need 7 volts to charge and 12 volt batteries need 14 volts to charge.

Chapter 9

Electric Starter Systems

Overview of the Electrical Starter System

The starter system has two circuits. One is the push button circuit (the small wires), and the other is the battery power relay starter circuit, (the big wires).

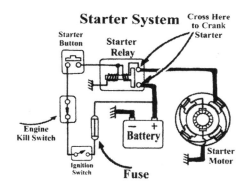

When the ignition switch is on and the kill switch is closed, pushing the starter button sends current to the starter relay. The starter relay is a magnetic switch that comes on when it gets current from the battery through the starter button.

The starter relays job is to close the starter power circuit. When the starter relay circuit is closed, current from the battery passes to the starter. When the starter gets the current from the battery, it cranks over the motor.

Did You Know That?

If your starter stops working while you are on the road, you can always push-start your bike.

Troubleshooting the Starter System

Read all there is to know about your starter system in your service manual before starting to troubleshoot your system.

The first thing you want to know is which circuit the trouble is on. Is it the push button circuit (the small wires) or the starter power circuit (the big wires).

When you troubleshoot the starter system, you begin by checking the fuse, then you go on to the starter relay. You begin here for two reasons; one is that it's usually easy to get to the starter relay, and two, it's the only place where the two circuits come together.

Begin by jumping the starter relay with an old screwdriver. This will tell you if the battery and the starter are in good condition. You find the starter relay by following the batteries large, positive lead to where it is bolted on to the starter relay.

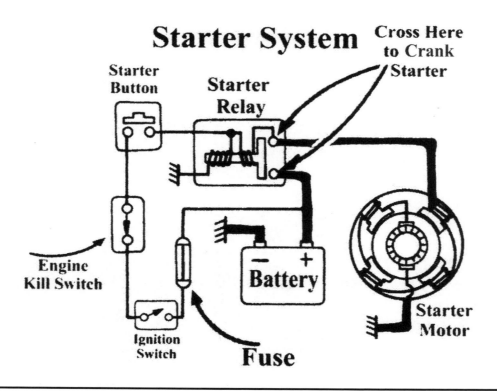

At the same place, you will see that the large lead that goes to the starter is also bolted to the starter relay. Cross the two bolt heads with a screwdriver. This will cause some sparking, which is no big deal as long as you're not covered with gas. (Safety Tip!)

If the motor cranks over in the usual way, you know that the battery and its lead wires and the starter motor are working. If the motor does not crank over, then there are only three possible problems: (1) the battery does not have enough power to crank the starter; (2) the starter is bad; or (3) the starter's leads are loose or disconnected.

The fastest way to check the starter is to take a different known good battery and a set of jumper cables and jump directly to the starter. When you put current directly to the starter motor and the engine turns over, then you know that the starter is good.

If the starter motor doesn't turn over, it's bad and should be replaced or rebuilt. If the starter is good and the starter circuit wires are good, then it's the battery that's bad, and that's a quick and easy fix – just buy a new battery and install it.

If the starter turns over when you jump the starter relay, then you know that the starter circuit (the big wires) is good and the problem must be either with the starter relay itself, or in the starter button circuit, (the small wires.)

Rule of Thumb

If the starter makes a lot of grinding noise when you push the starter button, you either have a bad starter or a bad starter clutch.

Next, test the starter relay. Unplug the two small wires coming out of the starter relay. Take a jumper wire and connect one end to the positive side of the battery and the other end to one of the starter relays small wires, (it doesn't matter which one).

Take another jumper and connect one end of it to the batteries ground and connect the other end of the jumper to the second wire coming out of the starter relay. When you connect the second jumper to the starter relay, the starter relay should close the starter circuit with a "click", cranking over the motor. If it does, then the starter relay is doing it's job. If not, the starters relay is bad and should be replaced.

If the starter relay is good, then the problem must be in the push button starter circuit itself. Take the ice pick tester and test each component in the starter push button circuit until you find the culprit. Then replace the bad component.

The wiring diagram in your service manual will tell you what is in your particular push button starter circuit. It will give you the colour codes, so you can trace the push button starter wiring.

Once you have fixed the push button circuit, then try starting the bike by pushing the starter button. It should start. If not, then start at the top of this chapter and go over the list again. When you can crank the bike over by pushing the starter button, then you're finished with troubleshooting the starter system.

In a Nut-Shell

The bare minimum of components that you need in an electric starter system is a battery, a starter, a starter relay and a push button that turns the starter relay on and off.

Chapter 10

Tune & Service

Overview of a Tune & Service

Now that you have gotten your motor up and running, would you like to keep it running? Yes? Good, then give it a good tune and service.

Unlike tune-ups on cars, a motorcycle gets a full tune and service. Cars get new spark plugs, an air filter (maybe), and an oil and filter change on request. The oil and filter change usually costs extra, and that's about it.

A motorcycle gets it all, from stem to stern; everything is done for safety reasons.

A motorcycle is more like an airplane when it comes to maintenance. Riding a motorcycle is more three dimensional, much more like flying an airplane than driving a car. That is why people love riding motorcycles, they get to fly and stay on the ground – most of the time.

Doing a tune and service is a skill you can learn, and it will save you a lot of time and money by doing it yourself.

How to Do a Tune & Service

First, take an overall view of the motorcycle to see if there is any obvious damage, or repairs that can be done during the tune and service. Then check the oil level, and add oil if needed.

4-Stroke Motor Tune-ups

The valve adjustment is done first and takes about 80% of the time of a tune and service. This usually includes removing the fuel tank, the side covers and seat, the fairing and anything else that needs to be removed to gain access to the valve cover (s).

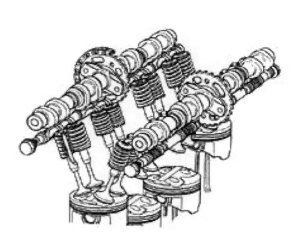

Remove the valve cover (s) and adjust the valves. See your service manual for the details on your bike. After the valves have been adjusted, and a new valve cover gasket has been installed (along with cam end plugs, if your bike takes them), put the valve cover back on and retorque the bolts that hold the cover on.

Adjust the valve timing chain, if necessary. See your service manual. Install new spark plugs and spark plug caps.

If the motor has a points ignition system, then the points are checked for misalignment, burning, or pitting. If needed, the points and condensers are replaced along with a new air filter.

If it's a liquid-cooled bike, then check the coolant level. Replace the coolant with new anti-freeze, if you don't know how old it is.

The motor is then started and the spark timing and advance are checked and or adjusted.

When the motorcycle is up to it's normal operating temperature and it is a liquid cooled bike, then check to see if the cooling fan is coming on when it is supposed to.

While the oil is hot, change the oil and the oil filter. We use Castrol GTX 20w50 and a Fram oil filter. Damn, they're still not paying us for that advertisement!

At this time, check and fill all liquids including the rear end oil, the brake fluids and the coolant.

Synchronizing the carburetors is next. Use mercury carb gauges, as they are the best in giving you a very accurate carb sync. See your service manual for details.

All the controls are inspected and adjusted including the throttle grip free play, the clutch lever and cable, the brakes (both front and rear), and the brake levers.

Check, adjust and lubricate the main drive chain (if it has one), if not, check the oil in the rear end.

Check all the nuts, bolts and screws for tightness.

Check that the tires are aligned and filled with the right amount of air pressure.

Test all the lights, including the headlight for high beam and low beam, the turn signals, the brake lights (both hand and foot) and the taillight.

Now it's time to take the bike out for a test ride and a safety check (see Safety Test). Anything that is not perfect is taken care of or is noted for future repair.

You can do your own tune and service. The entire how-to for your bike is in your service manual. Take the list given here as a guide and take your time. You will gain confidence and save a fortune over the lifetime of owning your motorcycle. You will save enough money to pay for all the tools you need by the time you do one tune and service yourself.

2-Stroke Motor Tune ups

Read how to do a tune and service on 4-strokes first. A tune and service is much easier on a 2-stroke than on a 4-stroke because 2-strokes don't have intake and exhaust valves that need adjusting.

- Change the spark plug and cap.

- Change the gearbox oil.

- If your bike has an oil injector, then fill the reserve.

- Check the brakes.

- Check all the levers and adjust them if needed.

- Check all the lights.

- Check the tires for the right amount of air pressure, and fill, if needed. Also, check and adjust the chain.

- If it has a radiator, check and/or change the coolant.

- If it has points, then check them and time the bike; then see if the timing advance is working correctly. Do a safety test.

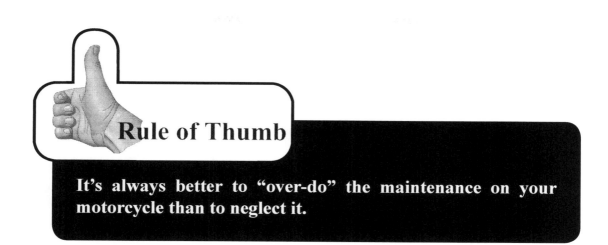

Rule of Thumb

It's always better to "over-do" the maintenance on your motorcycle than to neglect it.

Motorcycle Safety Check

First, make sure that the motorcycle tires are properly filled with air and the oil level is up. Do a tune and service first, (see above – Tune & Service).

The Safety Test

Sit on the motorcycle with the motor running and turn the handlebars from side to side to see if the rpm goes up; if it does, then the throttle cables need to be re-routed or adjusted.

The brakes are next. Roll the bike back and forth while applying the brakes to see if they are working. If they don't work properly, then fix them before riding the bike.

Check all the lights and turn signals as well as the horn. If they're not working correctly, fix them before driving the bike.

The clutch is adjusted to the one finger rule. This is where you put one finger between the clutch lever and the handle bar grip, pulling the clutch in and putting the bike into first gear. Then let the clutch out a little; the clutch should start to engage as soon as the lever leaves your finger. If not, adjust the clutch cable or the clutch adjuster until it does.

Take the bike out for a ride, checking the brakes again, as you go.

Once you have driven somewhere safe, with no one behind you, hit the brakes one at a time, as hard as you can without putting the bike down. This is an emergency braking test.

Go around corners to see how the bike handles.

Go up on a sidewalk and drop off the curb to check the front and rear suspension.

Last, but not least, after the bike is warmed up, do a "dynamic carb test".

Setting Up & Synchronizing The Carbs

When everything has been done right in a tune and service - the valves have been adjusted and you have put new spark plugs and spark plug caps on your bike; now you're ready to do the magic.

The magic is setting up your carbs and synchronizing them. What is synchronization? If you have more than one carburetor, then they have to be balanced so that they all work as a team. Balancing them is synchronizing them.

Every carb has to pull it's weight; we don't want one carb to start opening up sooner than the others, making that cylinder do more work than the others. We also don't want a carburetor to start to open late causing that cylinder to drag behind the rest. What we want is all the carbs opening and closing as if they were just one carburetor.

Before synchronizing and during synchronizing, the carbs need to be set up. Set-up means that the carbs are in good shape, working right and the spark plug colour is neutral. Neutral means that the spark plugs are not running too lean (white) or too rich (black) on the spark colour test.

The spark plug colour test determines how rich or lean your individual carbs are running. (See Chapter 11 - The Land of Experimentation). Carbs are synchronized at idle, so idle is the only rpm we're thinking about while synchronizing the carbs.

The spark plug colour test is done by putting a new set of NGK spark plugs in an already warmed up motor and running it at idle (1000 rpm) for five to ten minutes. Then the spark plugs are removed and if the tips are white, then they're running lean and the idle enrichness screw should be adjusted to let more fuel through to the motor. If the spark plug tips are black, then you're getting too much fuel and the carb's idle enrichness screw should be adjusted to let less fuel in.

If the spark plugs come out after being run, in a pre-warmed motor and they still look as though they're brand new, as if they haven't been run in the motor at all, then you're in the neutral range. This neutral range is the right fuel/air mixture range to start carb synchronization. (If you need to do this test more than once, to get into the neutral range, make sure you install a brand new set of spark plugs for each test that you perform.)

Once you have a neutral fuel/air mixture, set up the vacuum carb synchronization tools (find out how in your service manual) and start the motor. A mercury gauge gives a very accurate reading, because it pulls inches of mercury instead of bouncing a needle and you may want to purchase one for your own use.

Adjust the carbs so all the carbs are pulling the same amount of vacuum, and then re-run the spark plug colour test. You will have to go back and forth between the colour test and the mercury gauge to get both right at the same time. Also, you will need to keep adjusting the idle to keep it within range.

When the idle is right and all the carbs are pulling the same amount of vacuum and at the same time the colour test is just right (neutral), then you're done. When you have adjusted all three so they're perfect, you will have a much smoother running motor. Setting up and synchronizing your carburetors is magic to your motor!

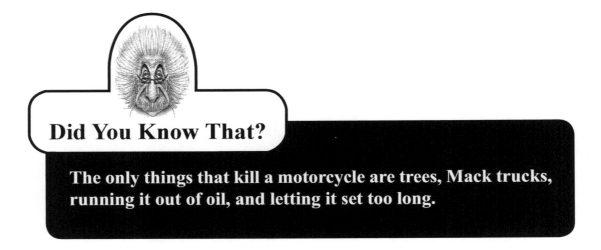

Did You Know That?

The only things that kill a motorcycle are trees, Mack trucks, running it out of oil, and letting it set too long.

Carburetor Power Test

After you have done the tune and service, which involved synchronizing the carburetors, you are ready to do the dynamic carb test.

This is a simple, but telling test that we invented that takes just a few minutes. The test will tell you what condition your carbs are in, along with the rest of the running ability of the whole motor.

Start by warming up the motorcycle to its full running temperature. Now ride the bike to a safe place with little or preferably no traffic. Slow the bike down to idle speed while traveling on a smooth flat road. At an idle, shift into third gear and snap the throttle wide open. What happens?

The bike should, very slowly at first, start to gain rpm. Without balking or sputtering, coughing or wanting to stall, it should move forward at a consistently increasing speed, until you reach into the high rpms.

If the bike does anything that doesn't seem right, then you need to find out why. It will usually be in your carburetors. If the bike takes off slowly and smoothly, and continues until it gets into the high rpms, then you can feel confident that all is right with your motor and carbs.

Remember that this test, not only tests the carbs, but the whole running system. If the bike has good compression and it has been tuned and serviced correctly, the only thing in the system that changes with rpm are the carbs.

If your bike runs well at one rpm and not at another, then the problem most likely, is in your carburetors. See Chapter 6 – How to Rebuild A Carburetor. If your bike runs well throughout the whole rpm range, then you know that your motor and carbs are in good shape.

In a Nut-Shell

You should tune and service your motorcycle a minimum of once a year and change the oil and filter every 1,000 miles.

SECTION III

124

Chapter 11

The Land of Experimentation

This section of the book deals with problems that haven't been solved by doing a "make-run" procedure and tuning it. Let's say that you have gotten your motorcycle up and running. You've done a good tune and service on it, and you have also rebuilt your carburetors and you know they're right. But your motorcycle still doesn't run right and you know it.

Ask yourself, "Has this bike been modified from stock?" Has the intake or the exhaust been changed from stock? If so, you're entering the Land of Experimentation.

When you change the intake to help the motorcycle get more air into the motor, you have also given the bike less gas; in other words, you have modified the air intake and changed the fuel/air ratio.

If your motorcycle was manufactured after 1980, it was running E.P.A. lean (see Chapter 6 on E.P.A Lean) from the factory to start with. If you have modified the intake, now it's running so lean that it may have a problem starting and running.

Has the exhaust system been modified? When you take off the stock exhaust system to put a hot set of pipes on, you are modifying the entire exhaust system. If you chop the pipes off, you are also modifying the exhaust system. Any time you modify the exhaust from stock, you are changing the fuel/air ratio.

Rule of Thumb

The manufacturers knew what they were doing when they engineered your motorcycle. If you modify the intake or exhaust, you had better know in advance what YOU are doing.

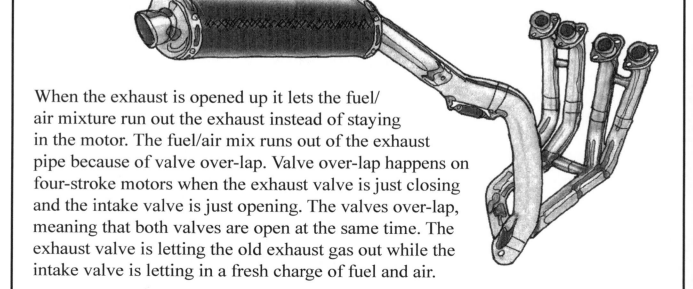

When the exhaust is opened up it lets the fuel/ air mixture run out the exhaust instead of staying in the motor. The fuel/air mix runs out of the exhaust pipe because of valve over-lap. Valve over-lap happens on four-stroke motors when the exhaust valve is just closing and the intake valve is just opening. The valves over-lap, meaning that both valves are open at the same time. The exhaust valve is letting the old exhaust gas out while the intake valve is letting in a fresh charge of fuel and air.

When this happens on a stock system, the exhaust system is designed to give a back pressure to keep the new fuel/air mix from going out the exhaust valve. But when you put a hot pipe on or modify the exhaust, you take away this back pressure. Some of the new fuel/air mix comes in through the intake valve and goes right out through the exhaust valve. The fuel/air mix that is left in the motor is then very lean, (too little fuel to air ratio).

An overly lean motor will pop, spit, and have lower power and run much hotter than a motor with the right fuel/air mixture. This can seriously damage the motor due to overheating.

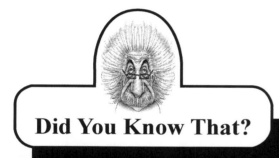

Did You Know That?

Are your mufflers rusted out on the inside, or does the exhaust system have holes rusted through? Then your exhaust system has been modified from stock by Mother Nature.

How do you fix it? Well you can put everything back to stock or you can enter the land of experimentation. You can change the carburetors to make up for the modified intake and the modified exhaust system, or both at the same time.

When you buy a new hot custom set of pipes, you should also get new jets that are matched to your motorcycle and to the new exhaust system. If it is too late to get a matched exhaust and jet system for your bike, or the stock exhaust or intake has been modified, then its experimentation time. In order to get the carbs to match the modifications to your system, you will have to re-jet the carburetors. Here is how to do it.

The spark plug colour tells all. A new spark plug should go in a warm motor and after running, it should come out neutral. Not white, which is too lean or black, which is too rich. It should come out looking brand new. You are in control of the spark plug colour.

Lets start with the idle test. Start the bike and let it warm up. Once it has reached running temperature, put in a new set of spark plugs. Start the bike, and don't choke it or run it past idle for ten minutes. Turn the bike off and take the plugs out. What colour are they?

If they're white at the tips, you're running too lean, so adjust the idle enrichness screw to let more fuel in at idle. Then repeat the test. If you don't have an idle enrichness screw, you can thank the E.P.A.

You will have to remove the carbs so you can get to the idle jet. Some bikes have E.P.A. cover caps over the idle adjustment screws that have to be drilled and removed in order to get to the idle enrichness adjuster screws.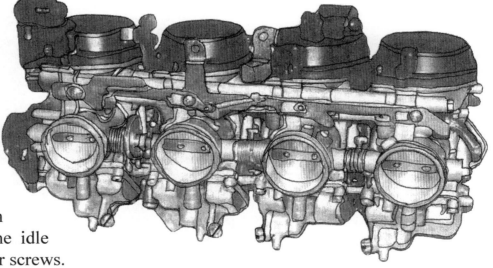

If your spark plug comes out black, then adjust your idle screw so you get less fuel at idle, or you can get a smaller idle jet from your dealership if you have an E.P.A. bike. Repeat this test, until you get a neutral spark plug at idle for all carburetors.

Next is your pilot jet, (slow jet). It handles the richness or leanness between idle and 2,500 to 4,000 rpm, depending on what year, make and model you have.

Warm the bike up and put in a brand new set of spark plugs. If your tachometer redlines at 8,000 rpm or less, run it at 2,500 rpm. If your tachometer redlines above 8,000 rpm., then run your rpm at 3,000. After five minutes, turn the bike off and take the spark plugs out.

What colour are the tips of the plugs this time? If they're white, they're too lean and you will need to drill the pilot jets out another drill bit size. If they're black, they're too rich and you will need to get smaller jets.

In this case, there is no outside adjustment. You will have to pull your carbs off the bike so that they can be drilled or fitted with smaller pilot jets. If you drill the pilot jets or replace them with smaller jets, you will also have to re-set the idle enrichness screws. See above.

Once you pull the carbs and you get the float bowls off, find the pilot (slow) jets. You will need to remove and drill the jets out one numbered drill bit size. After drilling out the pilot jets, reassemble the carburetors and redo the spark plug colour test.

What is the spark plug colour this time? If it is on the white side, then go back into the carbs and open up the pilot another drill bit size. Keep this up until you get a neutral plug colour or it starts running too rich, (black).

If you go overboard with the drilling and drill too big of a hole, then you should know what drill bit is just the right size. Get a new set of pilot jets and drill them to the last size that was not too rich. Once you have the pilot jets running with a neutral spark plug colour, then you're ready to go to the mid-range, the needle jets.

You do the needle jets test the same as the idle and pilot jets except that you do not drill the main jet. You raise or lower the slide needle to make it richer or leaner. Raising the needle makes it richer and lowering it makes it leaner.

Most motorcycles have an adjustable slide needle. If yours doesn't, then you will have to change the needle to change the richness and leanness. Thanks again to the E.P.A.

A faster taper and a smaller diameter, will make it a richer slide needle. A slower taper and a larger diameter slide needle will make it leaner. Once you have adjusted the needle and you get a neutral spark plug test, then start the test for the main jet.

Main jets are tested at 80% of red line. For example, if your bike redlines at 10,000 rpm, then you test the main jet at 8,000 rpm.

To test the main jet, warm up the bike and put in new spark plugs. Take the bike for a ride while keeping the bike at 80% of redline rpm for three to five minutes, (first gear will do). Then pull in the clutch and turn the bike off, gliding to a stop without the motor running.

Pull the plugs out right there (keeping track of what plug came out of what cylinder) and replace them with old but good plugs and ride home. When you get home, look at the plugs and check the colour and determine if they are running rich or lean. Drill or replace the main jets as needed.

If you make the main jets bigger by drilling them, then you will also have to go back to the needle jets and re-adjust them too, because the fuel for the needle jets comes through the main jets.

When you're finished, go back and re-check all the jets to make sure that you have a neutral plug in each R.P.M. range. In other words, redo all the tests.

Once you have a neutral spark plug throughout the whole rpm range, then re-do the carb set-up and synchronization. After the carb synch, do a dynamic carb test. (See Chapter 10 on Carburetor Power Test). When you get a good dynamic carb test, you're finished!

In a Nut-Shell

What is the point of all this? The point is, don't modify your intake or exhaust from stock, or else you will enter the Land of Experimentation!

Chapter 12

The Trade Secrets

Getting the Parts

Where you get your parts depends on what the parts are, that are needed. Some parts, should only be purchased new from the dealership that sold your brand of motorcycle. Some parts, on the other hand, can be purchased used. What is the difference?

Parts that come into contact with motor oil should always be replaced with new ones, as well as parts that are related to safety, such as your brakes, cables, etc.

Body parts, mirrors, fenders, seats, handlebars, lighting, rims, and almost everything that bolts to the frame can be replaced with good used parts. Electrical components such as lights, charging system parts, electronic ignition parts, coils, regulators, and wiring harnesses can be replaced with good used ones also.

Parts that should always be purchased new, are internal engine parts, tires, chains and sprockets. Incidentally, when changing chain and sprockets, always think of them as a set. You don't put a used chain on new sprockets, or vice versa. To do that, is to guarantee that you will have to replace them again just down the road. The reason? The old chain will wear on the new sprockets, or the old sprockets will wear out the new chain.

Save money on good used parts by buying a parts bike that is the same year, make and model as your own. For what you would pay for a new charging system for your bike, you can buy a complete non-running motorcycle that is a twin to your bike. You will have to search, but it is out there.

Remember that 80% of all bikes don't run and some people just want to get rid of them. Sometimes you can even get them for nothing, just for hauling them away.

If you're looking for used parts from a salvage yard, take your old parts in so you can match them up, because a lot of used parts places don't know what they have.

Some parts are interchangeable between years, makes and models. Parts such as mirrors, levers, and front brake master cylinders will fit almost all bikes from the same manufacturer of the same vintage.

When buying parts, make sure that you have the parts that you want before you leave the business, because sometimes they are not returnable. This is true for new as well as used parts.

No one will guarantee electrical parts, new or used. You buy them – you own them, that is just the way of it, they're not returnable. If you have to special order parts, expect to pay in advance for them.

So where do you get your parts?

1. The dealership.

2. A motorcycle salvage yard.

3. The Internet.

The Internet is becoming one of the best places to get both new and used parts. Spend some time on-line looking for your parts under new and used motorcycle parts. And don't forget eBay; there are people who make their living selling new and used motorcycle parts on eBay.

The Tools

If you don't have the tools you need to fix your motorcycle with, then borrow them if you can. If you have to buy tools, then just buy the tools you need.

We never buy kits of tools because 80% of the tools in a kit won't fit the nuts and bolts on any one motorcycle. So, just get the sizes you need for a particular job, or at least, for your particular bike.

Look at your motorcycle and figure out what sizes you will need and just get those sizes, unless of course, it cost less for a set of tools than it does for the individual tools you need.

Buy good tools. Sears Craftsman brand are okay tools; they will work if you're on a budget. Craftsman tools however, are as low down the list of tools as you should go.

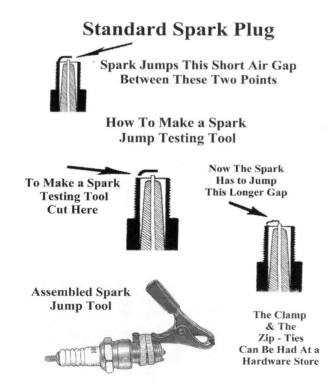

Standard Spark Plug

Spark Jumps This Short Air Gap Between These Two Points

How To Make a Spark Jump Testing Tool

To Make a Spark Testing Tool Cut Here

Now The Spark Has to Jump This Longer Gap

Assembled Spark Jump Tool

The Clamp & The Zip - Ties Can Be Had At a Hardware Store

For our own professional use, we like Matco tools, but all our ratchets are Craftsman, an old habit.

You will need sockets and extensions in the 3/8-drive size. We also use a 1/4 inch drive set-up for tight spots, and you may also need a 3/8 breaker bar.

Get open box-end wrenches that fit just the sizes you need for your motorcycle. Screwdrivers, both cross tip (Phillips) and flat tips. Again, get just the sizes you need.

Only get the specialty tools you need, to do a specific task. Get them from your local motorcycle dealership. Some specialty tools are no longer available for some older bikes, and you will have to make them or have them made. One tool you can make for testing your ignition system is the spark jump test tool and here is how to make it, shown on previous page.

You may need some of the tools that are shown on the next few pages. You will see graphics of the tools that we use most in our repair shop. We think that you should know what they are and how to use them.

Cable Luber:

The first one shown is of a cable luber. This tool is used for lubricating cables where it's easy to get to one end of the cable but not the other end. It lets you lubricate the whole cable from one end to the other.

Tone Generator:

The tone generator is a continuity tool. It has a battery inside of it and when you touch the alligator tips together, it completes the circuit and makes a high pitched tone. It's used for testing switches. You hook it to a switch and when the switch is turned on, (if the switch is good), the tone generator will sound. If the switch is bad, it won't.

Multimeter:

The multimeter is a multiple use tool. You will want one if you're doing electrical testing on charging systems, electronic ignition, or individual components when your service manual gives you a resistance test. It also does AC and DC output tests along with continuity tests.

Ice Pick Tester:

The ice pick tester is used for confirming that both positive and negative current is available. This is the first tool that we reach for when we're searching for an electrical outage. You use this tool by connecting the alligator clip to negative and testing for positive with the ice pick end. Conversely, you can test for negative current by placing the alligator clip on positive and searching with the ice pick tip for negative.

Float Adjustment Tool:

The float adjustment tool is used for setting the carburetor float height.

More Tools:

Hose Pliers:

We call the hose pliers, fingers, because they work as extensions of your fingers when you get into tight spots. They're great for pulling and replacing fuel lines.

Cutters:

You will definitely want to put your money into a good set of cutters – they're invaluable.

Magnet:

The magnet on a stick is a tool that you will want just in case you drop a bolt down a spark plug hole. Trust me on this one, you will WANT this tool!

Impact Driver & Tips:

The impact driver and tips is used for breaking loose those bolts and screws that have been locked in place by electrolysis. You put the right tip over the bolt or screw and twist it in the direction you want the bolt or screw to go in and then hit it with a heavy hammer. This tool drives and turns at the same time, breaking the bolt or screw loose. It's a must tool when you're working on older motorcycles.

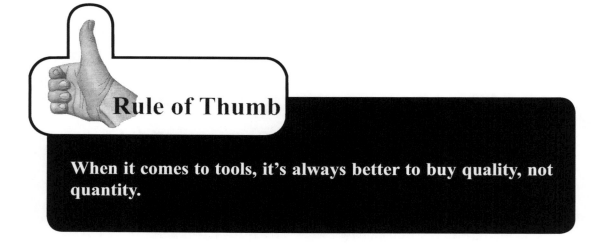

Rule of Thumb

When it comes to tools, it's always better to buy quality, not quantity.

Other Tools You May Need

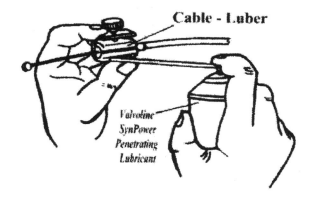

Cable - Luber

Valvoline SynPower Penetrating Lubricant

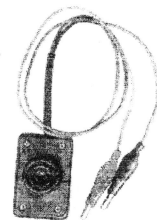

Tone Generator

Multimeter

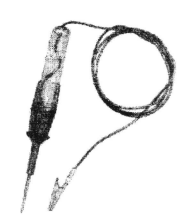

Ice Pick Tester

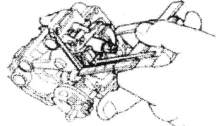

Float Adjustment Tool

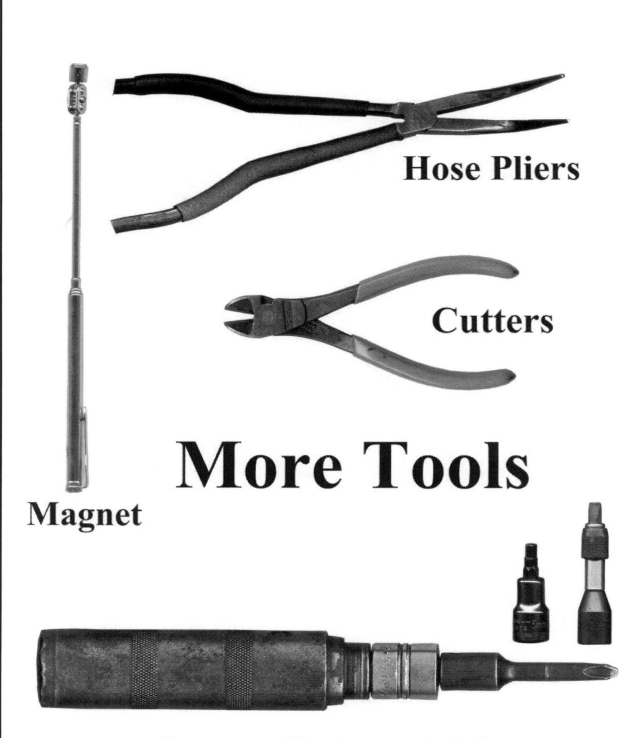

Hose Pliers

Cutters

More Tools

Magnet

Impact Driver & Tips

Now a word about the chemicals that are especially helpful. You already know about Mercury Power Tune Engine Cleaner, but there are other chemicals that are almost as useful as it. One that we use a lot of is WD-40. It's great for loosening up adjusters, such as your brake or clutch adjuster, and it's also useful for loosening up your carburetor linkage.

Valvoline SynPower Penetrating Lubricant is good when you need a lubricant that will last. We use it on cables, and especially chains and sprockets.

The last chemical tool that we're going to talk about is electrical contact cleaner. It's made by several different manufacturers and can be found (as all of the above chemicals) at most automotive supply houses.

Electrical contact cleaner is essential for cleaning points and electrical terminal connectors. It is also good for making plastic and rubber parts slippery to help in re-assembly of motorcycle components. For example, when you want to replace a set of grips on your handlebars, this chemical will greatly ease the job of installation. Just one word! Don't get it on you and don't breathe its' vapors – it's poisonous.

As you can see, it will not take a lot of tools to get a motorcycle up and running and you will pay for them in savings the first time you do your own "make run". In other words, it costs less to buy some tools and do it yourself, than it would to take your bike to a repair shop. Trust us here, we own a motorcycle repair shop.

Winterizing Your Motorcycle

There are several parts to winterizing (storing) your motorcycle.

The first is safety. Is the place where you store your motorcycle safe? Not just for the bike, but for the people that come into contact with it. A motorcycle can fall over if kids are playing around on it. Can your motorcycle possibly catch on fire where it's being stored? Just something to think about – and take action on.

The whole point of a winterizing list is to do what is necessary so your motorcycle will stay in the best condition while it's stored. You also want it to look good and run well when you take it out of storage, preferably without having to do another make-run procedure on it.

You see Mother Nature wants to turn your sweet baby back into it's natural elements. You know, all those things that man took from her to make your motorcycle. Mother Nature wants them back and she will eventually get them back. In the meantime, she is very patient, but if you don't take care of your motorcycle when it's stored, she will get a jump on you. Not to mention, that your motorcycle will not be as pretty as it was before you stored it and maybe it will not start when you take it out of storage.

We would like to tell you that after you finish with the list of details, that you need to vacuum-pack your bike, but we don't think they make vacuum packaging that big.

The list of details are for you to use, so your bike will continue to look good and start and run without you doing a lot of work on it after it's been stored.
You might think we are being a little rough here, but do you really want to go through another make-run procedure on your motorcycle? No, we didn't think so, so here we go.

1. Wash your motorcycle and make sure that you get all the dirt and road salt off of it.

2. Wax and polish all the painted and chromed surfaces.

3. If you have a main drive chain, wash and lubricate it.

4. Tune and service your motorcycle; this will save time and help it to start after storage. See Chapter 10 on "How To Do a Tune & Service".

5. If you have not started the bike in a while, start it and warm it up. This will make the whole engine happy.

6. Change the oil and filter. Change the oil while the engine is hot.

7. If you're not going to start the bike for weeks at a time, then remove the battery and service it. Then put the battery on a good trickle charger that will automatically keep the battery charged without over-charging it.

8. Store the fuel tank with fresh gas in it; it will go bad over the winter, but you can empty it in the spring into your car or truck. Storing the fuel tank FULL will prevent condensation from forming on the inside of the tank and rusting it. This step is only applicable if the fuel tank has NOT been relined. If it has, then this step isn't necessary.

9. Drain the fuel from the carburetors and the fuel lines.

10. Liquid cooled bikes should have their anti-freeze solution changed.

11. Use some chemical rubber protector on all the rubber and plastic parts.

12. Put a thin film of Vaseline on all the metal surfaces to prevent corrosion.

13. Check your tire pressure and fill with the correct amount of air.

14. Find a good safe place to store your motorcycle. Leave it on it's center stand and cover the bike. Remember, out of sight, out of mind. People are less likely to mess with a covered motorcycle.

15. If you can, start the motorcycle at least twice a month, and let it run for about 15 minutes at 2,000 rpm, this keeps all the motor parts working.

16. If it's a good weather day, take it out for a ride. It's the best storage procedure, and the best thing you can do for your motorcycle!

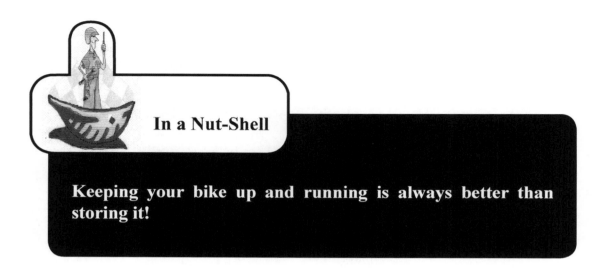

In a Nut-Shell

Keeping your bike up and running is always better than storing it!

Proper Start Up & Shut Down

Start Up

Some people over-choke their motorcycle when they try to start it, to the point of fouling the spark plugs. Once the plugs are fouled, they will never run right again. The choke is your friend until the bike starts, then it becomes your enemy!

The right way to start a motorcycle is to crank the bike over with the choke off for at least 10 to 20 seconds. This helps to clear the cylinders. Next, start to bring the choke on slowly until the motor starts. Hold the rpm up with the throttle and turn the choke off immediately. As long as it keeps running, keep the rpm up with the throttle. When it can idle, let it idle until it's warmed up.

If you don't do it this way, and you start it by using the choke to make it idle until it warms up, you are fouling the spark plugs. If you start your motorcycle this way, over and over, without letting the bike warm up, the plugs will foul to the point that the bike will not start.

In a Nut-Shell

Don't over-choke your bike. Use the throttle to warm it up, not the choke.

Petcocks

Some motorcycles have a vacuum petcock (the valve that turns the gas on and off). The petcock has three positions: "on", "reserve", and "prime". "On" is "on" only when the motor is turning over and "off" when it is not. The reserve is "on" only when the motor is turning over and "off" when it is not. Prime is always "on" whether the motor is turning over or not. This is controlled with the vacuum from the engine. Some motorcycles have just a plain on/off petcock and others have a plain on/off/ reserve petcock.

Shut Down

If you have control over the "on" and "off" on your motorcycle, you can do a lean shutdown. You do a lean shutdown because when a motor runs lean, it blasts the spark plugs clean. You do a lean shutdown when you're shutting the bike down for the day.

You let the bike idle, turning the fuel petcock off, letting the bike run until it runs out of gas. In the last few minutes, the bike will run very lean; this blasts the spark plugs clean of the carbon that was deposited when you choked the bike on startup.

Cleaning the spark plugs in this manner, makes starting the bike the next time, easier. Remember to turn the bike off after it stops running; most bikes will run the battery down if you leave the key in the "on" position.

The Secret to Keeping Your Motorcycle Running

Now that you have gotten your motorcycle up and running and you have fixed all the miscellaneous problems, do you want to keep it running, or do you want to do this all again next year? Silly question, isn't it?

Every time a customer leaves our repair shop after having a make-run done on his bike, and after paying the bill, we ask them if they want to know the secret to keeping their motorcycle running so they don't have to go through having a make-run done ever again.

They always say "Yes!" and we say that the secret to keeping their motorcycle running is TO KEEP IT RUNNING!

Setting kills motorcycles. Running them, keeps them alive. If you tune and service your motorcycle when you should, and run it, it will run forever.

Okay, maybe not FOREVER, but for every motorcycle that we have seen that has worn out, we have seen hundreds that have just set to death.

The secret to keeping your bike running is to keep it running. Do a tune and service on it at least once a year (or more, depending on how much you ride it). Your service manual will give you the tune and service schedule and we would recommend that you change your oil and filter every 1000 miles, we do.

In a Nut-Shell

Mother Nature will get all her natural elements back, sooner or later. Your job is to see that it's later rather than sooner!

Did You Know That?

Doing it yourself almost always pays off, even if you do it wrong. If you do it wrong, you can do it again until you get it right. In the end, you will have gained experience, knowledge and skill, not to mention an up and running motorcycle.

Conclusion

Okay, so you've read this book and hopefully you understand it. So, what have we done for you here? Well, you got information on how to get a service manual and specialty books to use for free through the Inter-Library Loan System.

We've walked you through the only logical procedure for getting a non-running motorcycle up and running.

We started with the compression, moved onto spark and then to the fuel system. If you had a problem with any of these, we walked you through all the troubleshooting processes.

We covered all the things that go bad when a motorcycle sets too long and how to fix them.

We covered the battery charging system, and how to get it working. The electric starter system was covered and we showed you how to troubleshoot it.

Tune and service was explained and a list was provided so that you could do your own tune and service in the proper order.

The Land of Experimentation was laid out so you would know what happens if your intake or exhaust was modified and what you could do about it so that your motorcycle would run well again.

We also covered all the trade secrets of getting parts, winterizing your motorcycle, proper start-up and shut down, and last but definitely not least, how to keep your motorcycle up and running so you will never again have to do another "make-run" procedure on it.

It is our sincere hope that this book has helped you in your goal to getting your bike up and running and to keeping it running right!

Randy Ellis

My Notes:

My Notes:

My Notes:

My Notes:

My Notes:

My Notes:

7722036R0

Made in the USA
Lexington, KY
12 December 2010